# the anti-ageing cookbook

## teresa cutter

NEW
HOLLAND

# Acknowledgments

My dearest thanks to the talented team at New Holland Publishers—Anouska Good,
Sophie Church and Nanette Backhouse—for making my second book come to life and
embracing my values and ideas for good, healthy, low-fat food.
Thanks to my husband, Paul, who produced the beautiful photographs; his eye for
detail and composition is reflected in each one.
Thanks too to Mark, Maggie and Lucy from Cyclops Films for being so patient and
understanding, and to Boris Mitchell from Kodak for assistance with the film stock.
Finally, thanks to Origin Homewares, Dinosaur Designs and Empire Homewares for providing
me with a wonderful canvas of plates and bowls with which to show off my food.

First published in Australia in 2002 by
New Holland Publishers (Australia) Pty Ltd
Sydney · Auckland · London · Cape Town

14 Aquatic Drive Frenchs Forest NSW 2086 Australia
218 Lake Road Northcote Auckland New Zealand
86 Edgware Road London W2 2EA United Kingdom
80 McKenzie Street Cape Town 8001 South Africa

Publishing Manager: Anouska Good
Project Editor: Sophie Church
Designer: Nanette Backhouse
Production Controller: Wendy Hunt
Reproduction: Colourscan
Printer: Kyodo Printing, Singapore

1 2 3 4 5 6 7 8 9 10

National Library of Australia Cataloguing-in-Publication Data:

Cutter, Teresa, 1968– .
The anti-ageing cookbook.

Includes index.
ISBN 1 86436 782 2.

1. Diet therapy – Recipes. 2. Longevity – Nutritional aspects.
I. Title.

641.563

**A note on measurements and ingredients**

Measurements in this book are provided, where relevant, in cups, grams,
ounces, fluid ounces and millilitres. One teaspoon is equivalent to 5ml,
and 1 tablespoon equals 20ml. Ingredients are listed using the names by
which they are most commonly known in Australia; alternative names are
as follows:

| | |
|---|---|
| Capsicum/bell pepper | Rockmelon/cantaloupe |
| Coriander/cilantro | Roma tomato/plum tomato |
| Eggplant/aubergine | Snow peas/mange tout |
| Papaya/paw paw | Spring onion/shallot |
| Red onion/Spanish onion | Tomato paste/tomato purée |
| Zucchini/courgette | Sweet potato/kumera/yam |

# contents

# Introduction: beauty comes from within

To a large extent, the way we look from youth through to old age is determined by our genes. We can't prevent our bodies changing as we grow older, or stop the ageing process, but we can at least slow down the effects of ageing through the choices we make about our lifestyle.

Three main factors play a significant role in helping us to grow old gracefully: nutrition, exercise and relaxation. Everything we eat and drink affects our overall state of health and wellbeing. By choosing natural foods that are fresh and pure, you will not only ensure that your body stays lean and fit, but you will also look better. Exercise will increase your metabolism and strengthen your body and immune system, making you trim and more resistant to disease; it will also boost your stamina and self-confidence, giving you plenty of energy and a better quality of life. If you exercise you will sleep better, and sleep and relaxation are essential for the body and mind to revive and recharge. Techniques such as deep breathing, yoga and meditation will help relax the body, reduce stress and improve your state of mind, and massage is excellent for improving circulation and skin tone and for relieving stress.

With regular exercise, enough sleep and a sensible, well-balanced diet you will look and feel healthy and energised. Your skin and eyes will be clearer, your hair and nails will be glossy and strong, and your body will be lean and toned. By boosting your stamina and self-esteem in this way, you can feel rejuvenated for the rest of your life.

## Why is a **healthy** diet so important?

Every day, we are all exposed to toxins in our environment from pollutants such as tobacco smoke, radiation and car exhaust fumes. Our foods are filled with preservatives, colourings and artificial sweeteners and our diets consist of highly refined and fatty foods. These all generate molecules called oxidants and free radicals, which can attack our cells and change or destroy their function. This can result in premature ageing, atherosclerosis (hardening of the arteries), heart disease, cancer, arthritis and other degenerative diseases. By choosing a nutritious diet consisting of foods rich in antioxidants (agents that combat or neutralise free radicals) we are much more able to maintain good health and slow the ageing process. Although the body produces its own antioxidants, our hectic and stressful lifestyles may mean the supply is diminished, which is why it is so important to consume good quality fresh foods.

# What are the top **anti-ageing** nutrients?

## Amino acids

Protein is broken down by the body into amino acids, which the body uses to build and repair cells. Amino acids are vital for our health and the correct functioning of our bodies.

**Good sources:** chicken · turkey · beef · seafood · eggs · skim milk · yoghurt · cottage cheese · beans · lentils · tofu

## Beta-carotene

Beta-carotene is a powerful antioxidant that can help neutralise free radicals in the body and stop their damaging effects on the cells. It can reduce the oxidation of fats in the body, which can cause a build-up of plaque in the arteries.

**Good sources:** red, yellow and green vegetables (e.g. carrots · tomatoes · sweet potato · red capsicum · cabbage · broccoli · spinach · peas · red chilli) · all orange-fleshed fruits (e.g. mango · rockmelon · papaya · fresh and dried apricots)

## Calcium

Sufficient calcium intake is vital throughout life. Calcium is important in childhood to ensure that superior bone mass is achieved and it is vital in adulthood to prevent osteoporosis in both men and women. It is also necessary for the proper functioning of muscles and nerves in the body.

**Good sources:** dairy products · dark green leafy vegetables · seaweed · tofu · sardines · salmon (including bones) · almonds · whole grains · seeds · pulses · nuts

## Coenzyme Q10

The coenzyme Q10 helps the body convert food to energy and strengthens the heart. It also acts as an antioxidant and plays a role in slowing down degenerative changes.

**Good sources:** animal organs · fish · vegetable oils · wheat germ · rice bran · beans · spinach · broccoli

## Folate

Folic acid is involved in certain biological reactions in your body and is necessary for the proper formation of blood cells. Deficiency in folic acid has been linked with fatigue, depression and heart disease.

**Good sources:** yeast extract · pulses (e.g. black eyed beans and soy beans) · whole grains (e.g. wheat germ and rolled oats) · fortified breakfast cereals (e.g. Special K) · oranges · brown rice · leafy green vegetables

## Omega 3

Omega 3 is an essential fatty acid. Research suggests it may help prevent cardiovascular disease, high cholesterol and heart attack, and may also prevent the onset of Type 2 (adult-onset) diabetes, some skin diseases and rheumatoid arthritis.

**Good sources:** fish (e.g. salmon · anchovy · mackerel · herring · sardines · trout · tuna) · nuts · seeds (e.g. linseed)

## Selenium

Selenium is an important trace element and powerful antioxidant that helps protect us from heart disease, some cancers and premature ageing. It also promotes healthy skin and hair.

**Good sources:** brewer's yeast · walnuts · lentils · sunflower seeds · broccoli · cabbage · onions · garlic · mushrooms · wholemeal bread · tinned tuna · sardines · salmon · swordfish · mussels · brazil nuts

## B Vitamins

These are a group of six water-soluble vitamins that are essential for the growth and proper development of the nervous system. They also aid the digestive system and help stabilise the body's metabolism.

**Good sources:** yeast extract · whole grains · sunflower seeds · nuts · nòri · eggs · poultry · nuts · mushrooms · oily fish · wheat germ · pulses

## Vitamin C

Vitamin C is a powerful antioxidant. Studies have shown that a high intake of vitamin C can dilate the arteries and improve circulation. It is also important for maintaining a healthy immune system and combating the effects of ageing.

**Good sources:** apples · pears · citrus fruits · blackcurrants · blueberries · kiwi fruit · strawberries · watermelon · rockmelon · mango · papaya · red grapes · dark plums · red cherries · red, yellow and green capsicums · red and green chillies · broccoli · brussels sprouts · green and red cabbage · lettuce · tomatoes

## Vitamin E

Vitamin E is a powerful antioxidant that protects the cell membranes from oxidation and helps to prevent the build up of plaque in the arteries, as well as thinning the blood. It helps to protect against heart disease and ageing.

**Good sources:** wheat germ · sunflower seeds · avocado · chick peas · tuna · salmon · spinach · brazil nuts · hazelnuts · almonds · vegetable oils · nuts · green leafy vegetables · cereals

## Zinc

Zinc is essential for healthy growth and development, fertility, wound healing, strengthening the immune system and healthy skin and hair. It also helps destroy free radicals in the body.

**Good sources:** wheat germ · liver · oysters · mussels · seeds · seaweed · nuts · beef

# What are the **anti-ageing** superfoods?

## Avocado

Avocados are high in fat, but much of it is the good monounsaturated type, which resists oxidation and helps to neutralise fat in other foods. Research also suggests that eating avocado lowers cholesterol levels. Avocado is a good source of vitamins $B_2$, $B_3$, $B_6$, C and E as well as potassium.

## Berries

Blueberries, blackcurrants, raspberries and cranberries all contain a whopping amount of antioxidants. Both blueberries and cranberries help ward off urinary tract infections.

## Broccoli

Broccoli provides an awesome array of antioxidants, as well as vitamins C and beta–carotene, which help protect against cancer and disease. It is also rich in folate and high in fibre. It is most effective when eaten raw or lightly cooked.

## Cabbage

Cabbages (including bok choy) contain anti-cancer and antioxidant compounds. Studies have shown that people who eat cabbage once a week have a 66 per cent less chance of developing colon cancer than those who eat cabbage once a month. It is also an excellent source of vitamin C and dietary fibre. Eat raw or lightly cooked for best results.

## Carrots

Carrots are high in vitamins A and C and a good source of dietary fibre. Studies have shown that eating a couple of carrots a day can lower blood cholesterol by up to 10 per cent. The beta-carotene in carrots acts as a powerhouse against ageing and disease. People with low levels of beta-carotene in their blood are more likely to suffer a heart attack, stroke or various cancers.

## Citrus fruit

The orange has been described as the complete package of natural anti-cancer inhibitors. An excellent source of vitamin C, which helps to make the collagen essential for healthy skin, it also helps maintain the body's defence against bacterial infections. Grapefruit contains a unique type of fibre, which studies have shown reduces cholesterol dramatically and helps prevent atherosclerosis (hardening of the arteries).

## Fish

Fish—particularly salmon, swordfish, anchovies, herring, mackerel, sardines and tuna—is the best known source of omega 3 fatty acid (see p. 6).

## Ginger, turmeric and black pepper

Ginger improves the circulation and helps prevent nausea, turmeric acts as an anti-inflammatory and antioxidant for the liver, and black pepper helps to stabilise blood-sugar levels.

## Ginseng

Ginseng is a potent herb used as a tonic for immunity, wellbeing and stress. Research suggests ginseng is beneficial in preventing premature ageing

## Grapes

Red and black grapes contain 20 known antioxidants that work together to fend off the free radicals that promote ageing and disease. The antioxidants are found in the skin and the seeds.

## Green tea

Green tea is rich in antioxidants. Studies show that people who consume one or two cups per day have a lower risk of certain cancers.

## Legumes

Studies indicate that regular consumption of legumes, in particular lentils and soy beans, reduces the risk of cancer. Soy beans are an excellent source of low-fat protein and can be found in foods such as miso, soy milk, tofu and tempeh.

## Onions and garlic

They might give you bad breath, but onions and garlic help prevent cancer, thin the blood by discouraging clots and increase levels of good HDL cholesterol. They also have anti-bacterial and anti-inflammatory factors that help keep colds and flu at bay. Next time you have a bad case of the flu, try eating a mashed raw clove of garlic sandwiched between two slices of bread. But make sure you do this on a weekend when you are not in contact with too many people!

## Red wine

A glass of red wine not only gives you a feeling of wellbeing, but research suggests it can also lower bad LDL cholesterol by as much as 46 per cent while increasing good HDL cholesterol by up to 24 per cent.

## Seaweed

The most common varieties of seaweed are kombu, wakame and nori. Seaweed is rich in essential minerals and contains an enzyme that helps to break down cholesterol. Studies suggest it may also be effective in helping to prevent a variety of cancers. Try to add kombu to all stocks, soups and casseroles to increase the nutritional value of the dish.

## Spinach

Spinach tops the list, along with other green leafy vegetables, as the food most likely to prevent cancer. It is a super source of antioxidants and is high in folate.

## Tomatoes

Tomatoes are the richest known source of lycopene, which gives tomatoes their red colour. Lycopene is more potent in cooked and canned tomatoes than in raw tomatoes. New research suggests that lycopene may help to prevent mental and physical dysfunction among the elderly and reduce the risk of prostate, pancreatic and cervical cancer.

## Water

Water is vital for life and helps the body to function at its best. We need to drink 2–3 litres of pure water every day to help with the processes of digestion, transporting nutrients and ridding the body of waste products. Many people tend not to drink enough water, which leads to dehydration, forcing the body to retain fluid. Dehydration can cause tiredness and lethargy due to the build up of toxins in the bloodstream. Drinking enough pure water is also an excellent anti-ageing tonic, as water helps the skin to stay hydrated, supple and fresh, as well as controlling the appetite and keeping hunger pangs at bay. When exercising, it is important to remember to increase water consumption to prevent dehydration, especially in hot weather. It is a good idea to drink before, during and after a work-out to replenish lost fluid stores. (The body loses about 2 litres per day through perspiration and breathing.)

# How can I make healthier food choices?

## Here is a list of high-fat foods with some healthier alternatives.

**Butter** Lecithin spreads, avocado, tahini, olive oil, low-fat mayonnaise, mustard, hummus

**Cake** Low-fat cakes made with wholemeal flour and unsaturated oils

**Salad dressings** Vinegar and olive oil, herbs, low-fat yoghurt, citrus juice

**Fried foods** Baked, grilled, poached or steamed food

**Hamburgers** Homemade burgers made from lean beef, fish, turkey or chicken mince, or veggie burgers made with lentils, beans or tofu

**Mayonnaise** Low-fat yoghurt, creamed tofu, cottage cheese, tahini, low-fat mayonniase

**Potato chips** Pretzels, rice crackers and vegetable crudités

**Sour cream** Low-fat yoghurt, tomato salsa, cottage cheese

**Vegetables with butter or high-fat sauces** Steamed vegetables with herbs and lemon juice, or stir-fried with soy or oyster sauce, or braised in chicken stock and seasoned with black pepper and garden herbs

**Omelette** Egg white omelette with mushrooms, herbs and tomato, or use 1 egg yolk for every 3 whites

**Whole milk** Low-fat or skim milk, rice milk or soy milk

**Cheese** Reduced- or low-fat cheese. or use a little of a strong-flavoured cheese, e.g. fresh parmesan

# How can I get **maximum** benefit from anti-ageing food?

Eating a variety of these superfoods is only half of the equation. The other half is being able to prepare them properly and simply without the use of too much saturated fat, and in a manner that will have little effect on their nutritional value.

The cooking methods used in this book are steaming, poaching, stir-frying, grilling, roasting, stewing and braising. These are the best methods for ensuring that foods retain as many of their essential nutrients as possible, and also ensure that the natural flavours of the fresh foods are enhanced, without the need for lashings of butter or high-fat sauces to heighten flavour. Vitamins B and C are water soluble, which means that boiling vegetables causes these vitamins to leach out into the water. Methods such as steaming and stir-frying avoid this problem. Stewing and braising are also suitable because the liquid used becomes part of the finished dish, rather than being discarded. Barbecuing and grilling are good methods of cooking fruit and vegetables as well as meat and fish, so long as care is taken not to overcook or burn food, as research shows that charred food may be carcinogenic (cancer causing).

When cooking any type of food, but especially fish, make sure that you do not cook it for any longer than is necessary. Protein foods such as meat and fish will become tough if overcooked, and flavours will not permeate the meat as readily. Overcooking also destroys some nutrients, particularly in vegetables, so try to ensure that vegetables are always served crisp and crunchy, and still brightly coloured.

Drinking fresh juices is an excellent, simple and convenient way of ensuring the body absorbs all the goodness of fresh fruit and vegetables on a daily basis in order to cleanse, build and recharge the body. For juices to deliver the maximum amount of nutrients, it is important to use the freshest produce possible. Use organic fruit and vegetables whenever possible or scrub well under cold running water to remove any pesticide residue. It is best to juice whole unpeeled fruits and vegetables, as many nutrients are stored in or just beneath the skin. It is also best to drink the juice straight away so that the oxidation process does not destroy essential vitamins and enzymes. See the Aqua chapter for juice recipes.

# Ten **anti-ageing rules** to keep you healthy and rejuvenated for life

*1*   Eat a variety of fresh, **natural** produce every day. This is the best way of ensuring you are getting adequate essential nutrients to nourish the cells. Always buy the best quality and freshest ingredients you can find (organic if possible), and do not store fresh ingredients for more than a couple of days (nutritional value in food decreases over time).

*2*   Eat regularly, but keep portions small and controlled. It is better to eat five or six smaller meals a day than two or three large ones. Concentrate on consuming most of your calories by mid-afternoon and choose a low-carbohydrate dinner. This way you will keep your metabolism **active** and stay lean.

*3*   Learn to keep cooking **simple** and light. The best low-fat cooking methods are steaming, poaching, braising, baking, grilling and stir-frying. Cooking without the use of too much fat and processed flavourings can help us enjoy the essence of good, wholesome fresh food.

*4*   Choose **low-fat** food. There is such an abundance of good low-fat produce available that there is no need to buy fatty foods ever again.

*5*   Moderation and variation are the keys to any **healthy** diet. Don't overload your body with too much of any one thing.

*6*   Drink, drink, drink. **Water** is vital for life.

*7*   Try eating in a calm and serene atmosphere. East slowly and savour every mouthful. This way you'll remain **relaxed** while eating, enjoy your food and your body will thank you for it.

*8*   **Avoid** foods that are highly processed and full of artificial colours, flavours and preservatives. Many low-fat products on the market are full of these, so read labels and be aware.

*9*   Make healthy eating and living part of your everyday **lifestyle** for the rest of your life. Remember there are no quick fixes to good health and wellbeing. A positive approach is the best way to achieve your goals.

*10*   Try to **exercise** a little every day for the rest of your life. Concentrate on strength work, flexibility and cardiovascular fitness.

# recharge

## breakfast food

# Breakfast couscous with sun-dried fruits and cinnamon soy milk

1 cup (200g/7oz) couscous

grated zest of 1 orange

1 cup (250ml/8fl oz) unsweetened apple juice

2 cups (500ml/16fl oz) calcium-enriched soy milk

1 cinnamon stick

1 cup (155g/5½oz) sun-dried apples, apricots and peaches, mixed

2 tablespoons chopped walnuts

apple juice concentrate (optional)

---

Mix the couscous, orange zest, apple juice, soy milk, cinnamon and dried fruits in a saucepan. Bring to the boil and simmer for 5–10 minutes until the couscous is swollen and tender. Spoon into serving bowls and top with the walnuts. Drizzle with a little apple juice concentrate if necessary.

Serves 4

# Honey coconut waffles with juicy mango and berries

1 cup (125g/4½oz) organic plain flour

½ cup (75g/2½oz) organic wholemeal flour

¼ teaspoon bicarbonate of soda

1 teaspoon baking powder

½ cup (45g/1½oz) desiccated coconut

2 cups (500ml/16fl oz) low-fat buttermilk

1 tablespoon pure honey

2 teaspoons vanilla extract

1 teaspoon cinnamon powder

2 free range egg whites, beaten to soft peaks

2 punnets (500g/17½oz) strawberries, washed and halved

juice of 1 lime

2 tablespoons apple juice concentrate

2 mangoes, peeled and sliced

---

Sift the flours, bicarbonate of soda and baking powder into a bowl and add the desiccated coconut. Gently mix through the buttermilk, honey, vanilla and cinnamon to form a smooth batter, then fold through the egg whites. Heat and oil a waffle iron and cook the waffles until golden.

Combine the strawberries with the lime juice and apple juice concentrate. Spoon over the waffles and serve with the sliced mango.

Makes 10 waffles

# Tropical Bircher muesli

1 cup (90g/3oz) rolled oats

2 tablespoons wheat germ

1 green apple, skin on, washed and grated

1 cup (250ml/8fl oz) unsweetened apple juice

1 cup (250ml/8fl oz) low-fat soy milk

grated zest of 1 mandarin

½ cup (90g/3oz) chopped sun-dried fruit (pears, peaches, mango and apples)

2 tablespoons thinly sliced brazil nuts

Combine all the ingredients. Stand in the refrigerator for at least 1 hour or overnight. Spoon into bowls and serve.

Serves 2

# Papaya and passionfruit yoghurt parfait

2 cups (440g/15½oz) peeled and chopped papaya

pulp of 4 passionfruit

1 cup (125g/4½oz) low-fat granola muesli

2 x 200g (7oz) cartons low-fat vanilla yoghurt

---

Combine the papaya and passionfruit pulp in

a bowl. Divide the mixture between serving

glasses and top with muesli and yoghurt.

Serve immediately.

Serves 2

# Blueberry and banana smoothie

2 cups (500ml/16fl oz) ice-cold skim milk or soy milk

1 cup crushed ice

1 tablespoon oat bran

2 heaped tablespoons protein powder

1 ripe banana

1 teaspoon honey

1 punnet (250g/9oz) blueberries

---

Blend the milk, ice and oat bran until smooth. Add the protein powder,

banana, honey and blueberries and blend well. Drink immediately.

Serves 2

# Blueberry hotcakes

½ cup (60g/2oz) organic wholemeal flour

¾ cup (100g/3½oz) organic unbleached plain flour

2 teaspoons baking powder

juice and grated zest of 1 orange

1 cup (250ml/8fl oz) low-fat milk

2 teaspoons vanilla extract

2 free range egg whites, beaten to soft peaks

2 cups (315g/11oz) fresh or frozen blueberries plus
extra for serving

1–2 teaspoons macadamia nut or grapeseed oil

pure maple syrup, for serving

Combine the flours and baking powder in a mixing bowl. Add the orange juice and zest,

milk and vanilla and mix to form a smooth batter. Fold in the egg whites and blueberries.

Heat the macadamia nut oil in a non-stick frying pan and pour in spoonfuls of batter.

Cook for 1–2 minutes on each side until golden.

Put the cooked pancakes on a plate, cover with foil and keep warm in a low oven while you

cook the rest of the mixture. To serve, layer onto plates and serve topped with blueberries.

Accompany with pure maple syrup.

Makes 10 hotcakes

*L110,894/*

# Rice porridge with banana chunks and honey

1 cup (185g/6½oz) short grain rice
grated zest of 1 oranges
4 cups (1 litre/1¾ pints) skim milk
1 cup (250ml/8fl oz) water
4–5 tablespoons fructose
pinch of salt
sliced banana, to serve
skim milk, to serve
honey, to serve (optional)

Place the rice in a heavy-based saucepan with the orange zest, milk and water.

Bring to the boil, lower the heat, cover and simmer for 20–25 minutes and

until the rice grains are tender and creamy. Add the fructose and salt. Spoon

into serving bowls and top with the sliced banana and honey. Serve with a

little extra milk and the honey, if desired.

This porridge can be made days in advance and stored in the refrigerator.

Reheat before serving, or it is equally delicious served chilled.

Serves 6

# Pumpkin butter

500g (17½oz) pumpkin, cut into chunks
¼ cup (40g/1½oz) dark brown sugar
½ teaspoon cinnamon powder
pinch of nutmeg
pinch of ginger
juice of 1 lime
1 teaspoon orange zest

Preheat the oven to 200°C (400°F). Wrap the pumpkin chunks in a piece of foil and bake in the oven for about 40 minutes until tender. While still hot, process in a food processor until smooth, then transfer to a small pan. Add the sugar, spices, lime juice and orange zest and simmer gently for 15 minutes until thick and smooth. Leave to cool completely. Store, covered, in the refrigerator for up to 5 days.

Makes 1½ cups

# Organic cinnamon fruit bread

500g (17½oz) unbleached organic plain flour
1 teaspoon sea salt
15g (½oz) fresh yeast, or 7g (¼oz) dried yeast
2 tablespoons sugar
1¼ cups (300ml/10fl oz) warm filtered water
2 tablespoons macadamia nut or grapeseed oil
450g (1lb) dried fruit (e.g. peaches, pears, apricots, sultanas)
80g (3oz) brazil nuts, sliced
1 teaspoon cinnamon powder

Combine the flour, salt, yeast and sugar in a mixing bowl. Mix well to incorporate the yeast with the flour. Pour in the water and oil and mix well for about 9 minutes until the dough is smooth and elastic. Cover the bowl with plastic wrap or a tea towel and leave in a warm place for 1–1½ hours until the dough has doubled in size.

Add the fruits, nuts and cinnamon powder and knead into the dough. Divide the dough into two portions and shape into freeform loaves, or place the dough into two 12 x 23cm loaf tins. Leave to rise in a warm place for 1 hour. Preheat the oven to 180°C (350°F).

Bake the loaves in the oven for 40 minutes until cooked through and golden. (Check the loaves after about 20 minutes and cover with foil if necessary to prevent over-browning.) Cool on a wire rack. Serve with pumpkin butter.

Makes 2 loaves

# Miso soup with rice, tofu and vegetables

4 cups (1 litre/1¾ pints) chicken or vegetable stock

1 teaspoon wakame flakes

2 tablespoons white miso paste

2 bok choy, washed and halved

1 red capsicum, sliced

2 cups (310g/11oz) cooked biodynamic rice

180g (6oz) silken tofu, sliced

> MISO *is a rich paste made from fermented soy beans. The two common types of miso are light (white) miso and dark (red) miso.*

Heat the stock and add the wakame flakes. Mix a little of the stock with the miso paste to dissolve then add to the soup.

Add the bok choy and capsicum and simmer for 2 minutes. To serve, divide the rice between four serving bowls and spoon over the soup, bok choy and capsicum. Arrange the tofu slices on top.

Serves 4

# Kedgeree

1 x 220g (8oz) can salmon

1 cup (155g/5½oz) cooked biodynamic rice

1 tablespoon chopped brazil nuts

2 tablespoons chopped coriander

4 hard-boiled free range egg whites, chopped

2 spring onions, sliced

1 red capsicum, finely diced

1 cup (220g/8oz) cooked sweet corn

juice of 1 lemon

2 teaspoons flaxseed oil

salt and pepper to taste

Combine all the ingredients in a bowl and mix well. Spoon into serving dishes and serve warm or cold.

Serves 2

# Apple and blueberry muffins

1 cup (125g/4½oz) organic plain flour
1 cup (125g/4½oz) organic wholemeal flour
1 teaspoon cinnamon
pinch of sea salt
½ cup (125g/4½oz) raw sugar
3 free range egg whites
1¼ cups (310ml/10fl oz) apple sauce
¼ cup (60ml/2fl oz) skim milk
¼ cup (60ml/2fl oz) macadamia nut or grapeseed oil
½ cup (60g/2oz) chopped walnuts
1¼ cups (250g/9oz) fresh or frozen blueberries

Preheat the oven to 180°C (350°F). Combine the flours, cinnamon, salt and sugar in a bowl and mix well. Add the egg whites, apple sauce, milk, oil and walnuts and mix until just combined. Gently fold in the blueberries. Spoon into prepared muffin tins and bake for 25–30 minutes until cooked through and golden. (Take care not to overcook the muffins to ensure they remain moist.)

Makes 12 muffins

# Banana bread

3 ripe bananas, mashed well
2 teaspoons vanilla extract
4 free range egg whites
2 tablespoons macadamia nut or grapeseed oil
½ cup (125g/4½oz) raw sugar
pinch of sea salt
1 teaspoon cinnamon
2 cups (250g/9oz) organic wholemeal flour
2 teaspoons baking powder
½ cup (60g/2oz) chopped walnuts
½ cup (90g/3oz) sultanas

Preheat the oven to 180°C (350°F). Mix together the bananas, vanilla extract, egg whites, oil, sugar, salt and cinnamon. Add the flour, baking powder, walnuts and sultanas and spoon into a prepared 21 x 11cm loaf tin. Bake in the oven for 40–50 minutes until golden. Cool on a wire rack.

Makes 1 loaf

# Tangelo, jasmine tea, fruit and walnut bread

½ cup (125ml/4fl oz) hot, strong jasmine tea

500g (17½oz) mixed dried fruit (e.g. sultanas, pears, apricots and peaches)

½ cup (125ml/4fl oz) pure honey

¾ cup (190ml/6fl oz) freshly squeezed tangelo juice (use oranges or mandarins if tangelos are unavailable)

grated zest of 2 tangelos

2 free range egg whites

2 tablespoons macadamia nut or grapeseed oil

2½ cups (375g/13oz) wholemeal flour

½ cup (30g/1oz) wheat germ

2 teaspoons baking powder

pinch of sea salt

½ cup (60g/2oz) chopped walnuts

---

Pour the hot tea over the dried fruit and set aside for 1 hour.

Preheat the oven to 180°C (350°F). Add the honey, tangelo juice and zest, egg whites and oil to the fruit and mix thoroughly. Fold through the flour, wheat germ, baking powder, salt and walnuts. Spoon into a large 12 x 23cm loaf tin and bake in the oven for 45 minutes until cooked through. (Cover with foil if the loaf browns too quickly.) Cool on a wire rack. Serve at room temperature.

Makes 1 loaf

# Grilled fruit on lemongrass skewers with vanilla yoghurt

2 lemongrass skewers, trimmed (or pre-soaked wooden skewers)

4 chunks of banana

4 chunks of pineapple

4 chunks of rockmelon

1 lime, halved

2 teaspoons honey

low-fat vanilla yoghurt, to serve

---

Arrange the fruit chunks on the skewers and place on a baking tray. Squeeze over the lime juice and drizzle with honey. Grill for 2 minutes and serve with low-fat vanilla yoghurt.

Serves 1

# Warm apples with berries and oatmeal crumble

2 cups (440g/15½oz) canned unsweetened
pie apple
2 punnets (500g/17½oz) mixed berries
1 tablespoon raw sugar
1 cup (90g/3oz) rolled oats
3 tablespoons maple syrup
2 tablespoons chopped walnuts
1 tablespoon macadamia nut or grapeseed oil
low-fat vanilla yoghurt, to serve

Preheat the oven to 180°C (350°F). Combine apple, berries and sugar and spoon into a heatproof serving dish. Combine the remaining ingredients and sprinkle over the top of the apple and berry mixture. Bake for 25–30 minutes until golden brown. Serve hot or warm with low-fat vanilla yoghurt.

Serves 4–6

# Spinach and herb egg white frittata

250g (8oz) low-fat ricotta
1 bunch spinach leaves, washed and chopped
1 bunch chives, finely chopped
1 teaspoon sea salt
black pepper to taste
10 free range egg whites

Place the ricotta in the centre of a clean tea towel or piece of cheesecloth, draw the edges together, then place in a colander set over a bowl. Weigh down with a heavy plate and place in the refrigerator for about 4 hours or overnight.

Preheat the oven to 180°C (350°F).

Combine the drained ricotta, spinach, coriander, chives, salt and pepper in a food processor and blend until smooth, then scrape down the sides and add the egg whites. Process for a further few seconds until combined. Pour into a baking tin lined with greaseproof paper and bake for about 40 minutes until set.

Remove from the oven and rest for 5 minutes before removing from the tin. Cut into wedges and serve.

Serves 4

# Melon with honey and lime

1 cup (220g/8oz) diced honeydew melon
1 cup (220g/8oz) diced rockmelon
2 cups (220g/8oz) diced watermelon
juice of 2 limes
1 heaped teaspoon honey
low-fat vanilla yoghurt, to serve

Mix together the diced melons and watermelon and divide into 2 serving glasses. Mix the lime juice with the honey and pour over the melon mixture. Serve immediately with vanilla yoghurt.

Serves 2

# Baked nashi pears with crunchy walnuts and sun-dried fruits

½ cup (60g/2oz) chopped walnuts

¼ cup (50g/1½oz) chopped sun-dried pears

¼ cup (50g/1½oz) chopped sun-dried peaches

zest of 1 orange

¼ teaspoon ground cinnamon

4 nashi pears, cored and scored lengthways or once around the circumference (use apples if nashi pears are unavailable)

3 cups (750ml/24fl oz) unsweetened apple juice

low-fat yoghurt and maple syrup, to serve

Preheat the oven to 180°C (350°F). Combine the walnuts, fruit, orange zest and cinnamon in a bowl. Fill the nashi pears with this mixture and place in a baking dish. Pour over the apple juice and bake for 15–20 minutes until the pears are golden. Serve warm accompanied by yoghurt and drizzled with maple syrup.

Serves 4

# Thick-cut toast with scrambled egg whites and sautéed mushrooms

100g (3½oz) mushrooms (e.g. shiitake, button), sliced
½ red capsicum, diced
1 tablespoon chopped chives
1 tablespoon low-salt soy sauce
4 free range egg whites
1 tablespoon water
sea salt and pepper to taste
2 tablespoons low-fat ricotta or cottage cheese
toasted wholemeal bread, to serve

Sauté the mushrooms in a non-stick pan with a little water until soft. Add the capsicum, chives and soy sauce and heat through. Set aside. Whisk the egg whites lightly with the water, salt and pepper. Heat a non-stick saucepan over a medium heat and pour in the beaten egg whites. Cook, stirring with a wooden spoon, gathering all the soft, moist curds until creamy. Fold through the ricotta or cottage cheese, then spoon onto the wholemeal toast and top with the mushrooms. Serve immediately.

Serves 1

# Ricotta, sweet corn and tomato quesadillas

1 onion, sliced
2 cloves garlic, chopped
½ teaspoon paprika
1 cup (155g/5½oz) sweet corn
1 red capsicum, diced
2 tomatoes, diced
2 spring onions, sliced
4 corn tortillas
cracked pepper
2 heaped tablespoons smooth low-fat ricotta or cottage cheese

Preheat the oven to 220°C (450°F). Sauté the onion and garlic until golden. Add the paprika, sweet corn and capsicum. Cook for a further minute, remove from the heat and fold through the tomato and spring onions.

Place two tortillas on a lightly greased baking tray and top each with the sweet corn and tomato mixture. Season well with cracked pepper. Spread the remaining two tortillas with the ricotta or cottage cheese and place over the top of the sweet corn mixture to form a quesadilla. Weigh down with a plate or tray to flatten. Bake for 15–20 minutes (with the plate or tray still on top). Cut into wedges and serve hot or warm.

Serves 2

# natural

rejuvenating
salads and
vegetables

# Borlotti bean salad with parmesan toast

1 x 440g (15oz) can borlotti beans

2 spring onions, sliced

2 cloves garlic, chopped

1 green capsicum, sliced

2 tablespoons chopped chives

4 tablespoons balsamic vinegar

good grind of black pepper

## Toast

2 thin slices wholemeal sourdough bread

2 tablespoons freshly grated parmesan cheese

Preheat the oven to 180°C (350°F). Combine all the ingredients and set aside. Sprinkle the parmesan cheese over the bread and bake in the oven for 10–15 minutes until golden. Remove, cool and serve with the salad.

Serves 2

# Crunchy green bean salad

220g (8oz) green beans, lightly steamed

2 tomatoes, quartered, seeded and sliced

½ red onion, sliced

2 spring onions, sliced

1 cup (250g/9oz) bean sprouts

cashew nuts and coriander leaves, to garnish (optional)

## Dressing

1 tablespoon chopped coriander

2 cloves garlic, chopped

2 teaspoons fish sauce

juice of 2 limes

1 red chilli, chopped

1 teaspoon honey

Make the dressing by combining all the ingredients. Mix well and set aside. Combine the beans with sliced tomato, onion, spring onions and bean sprouts. Pour over the dressing and toss well. Garnish with roasted cashew nuts and coriander leaves, if desired.

Serves 2

# Guacamole, cucumber and smoked salmon salad with chunky tomato salsa

100g (3½oz) smoked salmon, sliced
1 cucumber, peeled and thinly sliced lengthways using a vegetable peeler

## Guacamole

½ avocado, chopped
2 spring onions, sliced
¼ small red chilli, finely diced
juice of 1 lemon
pinch of salt and ground black pepper
1 tablespoon chopped coriander

## Salsa

2 tomatoes, peeled, seeded and diced
½ red capsicum, finely diced
½ red onion, finely diced
2 cloves garlic, crushed
juice of 2 limes
1 teaspoon sugar
sea salt and pepper, to taste

Combine the guacamole ingredients and mix well. Spoon onto serving plates using a round biscuit cutter as a mould. Arrange the slices of smoked salmon on top, followed by long strips of cucumber. Combine the salsa ingredients and spoon alongside the guacamole.

Serve immediately.

Serves 2

# Chickpea and vegetable curry with tofu

2 onions, sliced
4 cups (1 litre/1¾ pints) vegetable stock
4 cloves garlic, crushed
2 teaspoons curry powder
1 x 440g (15oz) can chickpeas
½ cauliflower, cut into florets
1 head broccoli, cut into florets
1 bunch spinach leaves, washed
2 tomatoes, chopped
300g (10½oz) firm tofu, cubed
steamed brown rice, to serve

Heat a non-stick pan over a high heat and fry the onions in a little of the stock until soft. Add the garlic and curry powder. Cook for 1 minute then add the rest of the stock, chickpeas, cauliflower and broccoli. Simmer for 5–10 minutes until the vegetables are tender. Add the spinach leaves, tomatoes and tofu. Heat through until the spinach has wilted and the tofu is warm. Adjust the seasoning and serve in bowls, accompanied with steamed brown rice.

Serves 4

# Biodynamic rice and tuna salad

1 cup (155g/5½oz) cooked biodynamic rice
pinch of sea salt and freshly ground black pepper
1 x 250g (9oz) can tuna in spring water, drained
1 yellow capsicum, diced
zest and juice of 1 lemon
2 cloves garlic, crushed
2 tablespoons chopped chives
3 spring onions, sliced
2 tablespoons chopped parsley
1 tablespoon chopped coriander
1 teaspoon fish sauce (optional)
1 tablespoon soy sauce
1 teaspoon sesame oil

Combine all the ingredients and mix gently. Store, covered, in the refrigerator until ready to serve.

Serves 2

# Gado gado with tofu

250g (9oz) asparagus
2 carrots, peeled and cut into sticks
2 red capsicums, sliced
2 yellow capsicums, sliced
1 Lebanese cucumber, cut into sticks
155g (5½oz) snow peas
155g (5½oz) bean sprouts
440g (15oz) firm tofu
1 iceberg lettuce

## Peanut sauce

1 onion, diced
4 cloves garlic, crushed
1 red chilli, seeded and diced
4 heaped tablespoons peanut butter
2 tablespoons low-salt soy sauce
1 cup (250ml/8fl oz) water
½ cup (125ml/4fl oz) low-fat coconut milk

First make the peanut sauce. Cook the onion, garlic and chilli in a little water until softened. Add the peanut butter, soy sauce, water and coconut milk and cook over a low heat until combined. Mix together the raw vegetables and tofu. Fill iceberg lettuce leaves with the mixture. Spoon over a little peanut sauce and serve.

Serves 6

# Chilli chicken salad with cucumber and roasted cashew nuts

90g (3oz) poached chicken meat

1 handful baby spinach leaves, washed and dried

15g (½oz) watercress leaves

½ red onion, thinly sliced

1 red capsicum, sliced

1 spring onion, sliced

30g (1oz) sliced cucumber

2 tablespoons chopped coriander

2 tablespoons chopped roasted cashew nuts

## Dressing

1 clove garlic, crushed

1 red chilli, diced

juice of 2 limes

2 teaspoons fish sauce

2 teaspoons soy sauce

1 teaspoon honey

Make the dressing by mixing together the garlic and chilli. Add the lime juice, fish sauce, soy sauce and honey and mix well. Set aside. Tear the cooked chicken into pieces and place in a bowl. Add the remaining ingredients, pour over the dressing and mix well.

Serves 1

# Steamed vegetables with wakame and miso sesame dressing

500g (17½oz) assorted vegetables (e.g. snow peas, baby corn, broccoli, asparagus, bok choy, zucchini, carrot)

1 tablespoon dried wakame

## Dressing

1 tablespoon white miso paste

1 tablespoon low-salt soy sauce

1 teaspoon sesame oil

1 tablespoon mirin

4 tablespoons water

Wash the vegetables well and cut into equal-sized pieces. Steam for about 5 minutes until just tender. Meanwhile, soak the wakame in a little hot water for 3 minutes until soft. Combine the dressing ingredients and set aside.

Divide the steamed vegetables between serving plates, drain the wakame and arrange over the vegetables, then pour over the dressing.

Serves 2

# Raw energy salad

1 raw beetroot, grated
1 raw carrot, grated
1 whole head of broccoli, finely chopped
¼ Savoy cabbage, finely shredded
3 spring onions, sliced
2 cloves garlic, crushed
2 tablespoons pumpkin seeds
2 tablespoons chopped walnuts
2 tablespoons chopped parsley

## Dressing

3 tablespoons red wine vinegar
1 teaspoon wholegrain mustard
2 tablespoons olive oil
sea salt and pepper

Combine the dressing ingredients, mix well and set aside. In a large bowl, mix the salad ingredients and pour the dressing over the top. Toss well and serve.

Serves 4–6

# Baby spinach leaves with roasted pumpkin, walnuts and mandarin lime dressing

500g (17½oz) pumpkin, cut into cubes

1 bunch baby spinach leaves, washed

1 punnet cherry tomatoes, halved

2 spring onions, sliced

2 tablespoons chopped parsley

2 tablespoons chopped walnuts

### Dressing

zest and juice of 1 mandarin

juice of 1 lime

1 tablespoon cold-pressed olive oil

sea salt and black pepper, to taste

Preheat the oven to 220°C (425°F). Roast the pumpkin in the oven for 30 minutes or until cooked through. Allow to cool to room temperature then combine with the spinach, tomatoes, spring onions, parsley and walnuts. Combine the dressing ingredients and pour over the pumpkin salad. Toss well and serve.

Serves 2–4

# Warm smashed sweet potato with mustard seed dressing, crunchy walnuts and peas

500g (17½oz) sweet potato (unpeeled)
1 teaspoon sea salt
1 teaspoon freshly-ground black pepper
2 spring onions, sliced
2 tablespoons chopped parsley
1 cup (155g/5oz) green peas, cooked
2 tablespoons chopped walnuts

### Dressing
2 teaspoons wholegrain mustard
4 tablespoons balsamic vinegar
black pepper to taste

Cut the sweet potato into chunks, place in a saucepan and cover with water. Add the salt and bring to the boil. Cook over a medium heat for about 20 minutes until tender. Drain well and lightly smash with a fork, including the skin. Place in a serving bowl, add the black pepper, spring onion, parsley, peas and walnuts and mix to combine. Combine the dressing ingredients and pour over the top. Toss well and serve.

Serves 4

# Warm vegetable pies

500g (17½oz) pumpkin, cut into cubes
sea salt and pepper, to taste
1 leek, washed and diced
1 onion, diced
2 cloves garlic, crushed
2 medium zucchini, grated
500g (17½oz) sweet corn
250g (9oz) shiitake mushrooms, sliced
1 red capsicum, finely diced
1 yellow capsicum, finely diced
2 tablespoons white miso paste
1 cup (250ml/8fl oz) hot water
2 tablespoons chopped chives
1 packet filo pastry
olive oil spray

Preheat the oven to 200°C (400°F). Place the pumpkin on a baking tray and season with a little sea salt and pepper. Bake for 30 minutes until soft and golden. Set aside to cool on the tray.

Sauté the leek, onion and garlic in a little water until soft and golden. Add the zucchini, sweet corn, mushrooms and capsicums. Combine the miso with the hot water and add to the leek and onion mixture. Cook over a medium heat for 10–15 minutes until the vegetables are cooked and the liquid has almost evaporated. Remove from the heat and mix in the pumpkin and chives.

Spoon into individual pie dishes and top with 1 sheet scrunched up filo pastry. Spray with a little olive oil and bake in the oven for 30 minutes until golden. Serve hot.

Serves 6–8

# Salad leaves with crisp pear, avocado and walnut dressing

6 large handfuls mixed salad leaves, washed and dried

1 pear, washed and sliced

½ avocado, thinly sliced

## Dressing

4 tablespoons apple cider vinegar

1 teaspoon cold-pressed olive oil

2 tablespoons chopped walnuts

1 teaspoon Dijon mustard

1 teaspoon sugar, or to taste

freshly ground black pepper, to taste

---

# Crisp green salad

1 cucumber, grated

1 small green papaya, grated

1 green capsicum, thinly sliced

2 spring onions, sliced

2 cloves garlic, crushed

2 tablespoons chopped roasted cashew nuts

2 teaspoons honey

1 tablespoon low-salt soy sauce

juice of 2 limes

---

Place the salad leaves in a large salad bowl. Add the sliced pear. Combine the dressing ingredients and pour over the salad. Toss well. Garnish with thinly sliced avocado and serve.

Serves 4

Combine all the ingredients and serve.

Serves 2

# Spinach and wakame salad with avocado, cucumber and miso vinaigrette

2 bunches spinach leaves, washed

3 tablespoons dried wakame

1 cucumber, peeled and thickly sliced

½ avocado, cut into even-sized chunks

1 tablespoon sesame seeds

### Vinaigrette

2 teaspoons white miso

1 tablespoon mirin

juice of 1 lime

½ teaspoon sesame oil

1 tablespoon low-salt soy sauce

1 tablespoon water

Plunge the spinach briefly in boiling water until just wilted. Drain immediately, plunge in a bowl of iced water, then drain again. Place wakame in a bowl and pour over 1 cup (250ml/8fl oz) boiling water. Leave to soak for 5 minutes. Remove the wakame from the water and combine with the spinach. Squeeze out excess water.

Take a handful of the mixture and place along the shorter edge of a sushi mat lined with plastic wrap. Using the mat, carefully roll up the spinach mixture to form a cylinder. Remove the mat and plastic wrap and cut the cylinder into 6–8 portions. Repeat until all the mixture has been used. Alternatively, form walnut-sized mounds of the spinach mixture with your hands.

Place the cucumber slices onto serving plates, then top each round with a portion of spinach and finally a small piece of avocado. Sprinkle with sesame seeds. Combine the vinaigrette ingredients and serve alongside the salad.

Serves 2–4

WAKAME *is a seaweed with a delicate texture. It is rich in essential minerals.*

the anti-ageing cookbook

44

natural

# Zucchini and watercress fritters with carrot and sesame salad

### Salad

1 large carrot, grated
1 teaspoon sesame seeds
1 handful watercress leaves
1 teaspoon olive oil
juice of ½ lemon
pinch of sugar

### Fritters

3 large zucchini, grated
2 tablespoons chopped coriander
1 handful chopped watercress leaves
2 spring onions, sliced
grated zest of 1 lemon
4 free range egg whites
3 tablespoons plain flour
sea salt and pepper
1 teaspoon sugar
1–2 tablespoons olive oil

First make the salad by combining all the ingredients, then set aside.

Combine the zucchini, coriander, watercress, spring onions and lemon zest. Add the egg whites and plain flour then season with salt, pepper and sugar. Heat a non-stick frying pan and brush with a little olive oil. Place spoonfuls of the zucchini mixture in the frying pan and cook for 2 minutes each side until crisp and golden. Serve warm accompanied with the carrot salad.

Makes 12 fritters

# Cool chicken rice paper rolls with chilli dipping sauce

2 tablespoons soy sauce

2 cloves garlic, crushed

juice of 1 lime

310g (11oz) poached chicken breast, cooled and shredded

12 large sheets rice paper (available from Asian grocers)

250g (9oz) iceberg lettuce, thinly shredded

1 Lebanese cucumber, peeled and cut into 5cm lengths

250g (9oz) bean sprouts

3 tablespoons chopped chives

2 spring onions, sliced

## Dipping sauce

2 cloves garlic, crushed

2 tablespoons chilli sauce

1 tablespoon chopped coriander

1 tablespoon fish sauce

1 teaspoon sesame oil

1 teaspoon honey

juice of 2 limes

dash of soy sauce

**LEBANESE CUCUMBERS** *are long and narrow with smooth skin. If unavailable, substitute a regular cucumber.*

Mix the soy sauce, garlic and lime juice, add the chicken and leave to marinate for about 10 minutes.

Soak the rice paper in hot water for a few minutes to soften and arrange the sheets on a work surface.

Arrange a little lettuce in the centre of each sheet, and top with some cucumber, bean sprouts, chives and spring onion. Finally, add some marinated chicken. Roll up each sheet, tucking in the edges half-way through rolling. Place in the refrigerator to chill.

Make the dipping sauce by combining all the ingredients, and serve with the chilled chicken rolls.

Makes 12 rolls

natural

# Oven-roasted red and yellow capsicums with basil pesto

2 red capsicums

2 yellow capsicums

400g (14oz) low-fat ricotta

4 tomatoes, quartered

sea salt and pepper, to taste

30g (1oz) shaved parmesan cheese, to garnish

### Basil pesto

1 bunch fresh basil leaves

juice of 1 lemon

3 cloves garlic, crushed

grind of black pepper and pinch of sea salt

4 tablespoons cold-pressed extra virgin olive oil

4 tablespoons chicken stock

1 tablespoon pine nuts, toasted

Make the pesto by blending all the ingredients in a food processor, adding a little more olive oil if necessary.

Set aside. Preheat the oven to 180°C (350°F).

Slice the capsicums in half lengthways and remove the seeds but leave the stem intact. Place on baking trays and spoon 1 teaspoon pesto into each cavity. Divide the ricotta between the 8 halves then arrange the tomatoes over the top. Season with salt and pepper and bake in the oven for 25–30 minutes until the capsicums have slightly collapsed and the tomatoes are soft and roasted.

Remove from the oven and place on serving plates. Drizzle with a little more pesto and garnish with the shaved parmesan. Serve warm with a large green salad or as an accompaniment to grilled chicken or fish.

Serves 4

# Pepper-crusted tuna salad

1 bunch baby spinach leaves

½ bunch watercress leaves

4 Roma tomatoes, quartered

1 red onion, sliced

200g (6½oz) snow peas, trimmed

2 x 200g (7oz) tuna steaks

2 tablespoons freshly ground black pepper

1 tablespoon fresh basil leaves, to garnish

## Dressing

2 cloves garlic, crushed

juice of 1 lemon

3 anchovies, crushed

pinch of sugar

1 teaspoon olive oil

Combine the spinach, watercress, tomatoes, onion, olives and snow peas in a large serving bowl. Coat the tuna steaks with the black pepper and sear in a little olive oil in a frying pan over a high heat, on both sides until just cooked through. Break up into pieces and combine with the salad ingredients. Combine all the dressing ingredients and pour over the tuna and salad. Toss well and garnish with fresh basil leaves.

Serve immediately.

Serves 4

# Stir-fried vegetables

1 onion, sliced

1 carrot, peeled and thinly sliced

¼ cup (60ml/2fl oz) vegetable stock or water

1 head broccoli, cut into florets

1 cup (155g/5½oz) snow peas

1 cup (90g/3oz) bean sprouts

2 tablespoons soy sauce

1 tablespoon oyster sauce

1 tablespoon roasted cashew nuts

Heat a wok over a high heat for 1 minute.

Stir-fry the onion and carrot for 2 minutes in a little stock or water until softened. Add the broccoli and cook for a further minute. Add the snow peas, bean sprouts, soy and oyster sauces and cashews. Warm through for 1 minute and serve immediately.

Serves 2

# strength

energising
food

# Oven-roasted cajun chicken with black-eyed peas

1 tablespoon paprika
1 teaspoon chilli powder
1 teaspoon ground cumin
½ teaspoon garlic powder
1 teaspoon curry powder
1 teaspoon ground black pepper
1 teaspoon ground coriander
4 x skinless chicken breast fillets
1 teaspoon olive oil
1 onion, diced
3 cloves garlic, chopped
2 cups (440g/15½oz) black-eyed peas, cooked
1 cup (220g/8oz) sweet corn kernels, cooked
1 red capsicum, diced
1 yellow capsicum, diced
2 spring onions, sliced
2 tomatoes, diced
3 tablespoons chopped coriander
2 tablespoons sweet chilli sauce

Preheat the oven to 200°C (400°F). Combine the spices and rub over the chicken breasts. Cover and marinate in the refrigerator for 2 hours.

Heat the olive oil in a pan and sear the chicken breasts on both sides until golden. Place in a hot oven to roast for 10–15 minutes until cooked through.

Meanwhile, sauté the onion and garlic in a little water until golden. Add the black-eyed peas, corn and capsicums and cook for 5 minutes until heated through. Mix in the spring onions, tomatoes, coriander and sweet chilli sauce. Spoon onto serving plates and top with the chicken breast. Serve garnished with extra sliced capsicum and spring onion.

Serves 4

# Red veal curry

2 onions, sliced

⅔ cup (160ml/5fl oz) beef or chicken stock

3 teaspoons red curry paste (see recipe, p. 157)

400g (14oz) lean veal steak, thinly sliced

2 red capsicums sliced

4 tomatoes, peeled, seeded and diced

1 teaspoon fish sauce

2 tablespoons light soy sauce

zest of 1 lime

2 tablespoons chopped coriander

⅔ cup (160ml/5fl oz) low-fat coconut milk

steamed jasmine rice, to serve

---

Heat a non-stick pan over a high heat and add the onions. Dry fry for 2 minutes until the pan starts to brown, then add a little of the stock and the curry paste. Cook for 1 minute over a moderately high heat. Add the veal, followed by the remaining stock and the capsicum. Simmer for 3 minutes until the veal is cooked. Add the diced tomatoes, fish and soy sauces followed by the lime zest, coriander and coconut milk.

Serve in bowls accompanied with steamed jasmine rice to soak up the juices (if you prefer a thicker sauce, add a little cornflour mixed with water and stir over a low heat until the sauce thickens).

Serves 4

# Silken tofu with bean sprout salad

300g (10½oz) firm silken tofu

155g (5½oz) bean sprouts

2 tablespoons coriander leaves

1 teaspoon sesame oil

2 cloves garlic, crushed

juice of 1 lemon

black pepper to taste

low-salt soy sauce, to garnish

---

Cut the tofu into cubes and divide between 2 serving bowls, leaving space in the middle for the salad. Combine the remaining ingredients and pile in the middle of the tofu. Drizzle over the soy sauce and serve.

Serves 2

the anti-ageing cookbook

# Tofu with chilled glass noodles

125g (4oz) glass noodles (bean thread vermicelli)
4 cups (1 litre/1½ pints) boiling water
2 cloves garlic, crushed
1 teaspoon sesame oil
2 tablespoons fish sauce
315g (10oz) firm silken tofu, cubed
handful of chives, chopped or whole, to garnish
low-salt soy sauce, to serve

Put the glass noodles in a bowl and pour over the boiling water. Allow to rest until the water cools. Drain well and toss through the garlic, sesame oil and fish sauce. Place in bowls or onto ceramic Asian-style soup spoons. Place the tofu on top and garnish with the chives. Serve with soy sauce.

Serves 2

# Baked cod with snow pea salad, roasted tomato and garlic

4 whole garlic bulbs
4 roma tomatoes, halved
1–2 teaspoons olive oil
sea salt and pepper to taste
4 x 185g (6½oz) cod fillets

### Snow pea salad

2 cloves garlic, crushed
2 teaspoons fish sauce
juice of 2 limes
1–2 red chillies, chopped
1 teaspoon honey
155g (5½oz) snow peas, sliced
1 red onion, sliced
2 spring onions, sliced
1 cup (90g/3oz) bean sprouts

Preheat the oven to 200°C (400°F). Wrap the whole garlic bulbs in foil and bake for about 35 minutes until softened. Meanwhile, place the tomato halves on a baking tray, cut side up, brush with a little olive oil and season well with salt and pepper. Oven roast for 15–20 minutes until slightly collapsed and browned. Brush the cod fillets with a little olive oil and season with salt and pepper. Sear on one side in a hot pan until brown, then turn over to sear the other side. Place the pan in the oven for about 6–8 minutes to complete the cooking.

Meanwhile, make the salad by combining the garlic, fish sauce, lime juice, chilli and honey. Add the remaining ingredients and toss. Arrange a piece of cod, two tomato halves, a whole garlic bulb and some snow pea salad on each plate and serve.

Serves 4

# Mussels with tomato and chilli

1 onion, finely diced

3 cloves garlic, chopped

1 red chilli, finely chopped

2 x 440g (15oz) cans puréed tomatoes or 1kg (2¼ lb) peeled and puréed fresh tomatoes

2 tablespoons tomato paste

¼ cup (60ml/2fl oz) red wine

2 teaspoons sugar

2kg (4½ lb) mussels, cleaned and bearded

2 tablespoons chopped parsley

1 tablespoon shredded basil

salt and pepper, to taste

crusty wholegrain bread, to serve

Sauté the onion, garlic and chilli in a little water until soft. Add the tomato purée, tomato paste, wine and sugar. Cover and simmer gently for 20 minutes. Add the mussels and cook for a further 5 minutes until opened. Discard any mussels that remain closed. Mix through the chopped herbs and season with salt and pepper. Serve immediately accompanied with crusty, wholegrain bread.

Serves 4

# Baked lobster tails with bean shoot and watercress salad and lime dressing

4 whole uncooked lobsters

1 tablespoon olive oil

100ml (10fl oz) sake or white wine

sea salt and ground black pepper

2 cups (250g/9oz) bean shoots, washed

1 cup (30g/1oz) watercress leaves

**SAKE** *is a Japanese alcoholic drink brewed from rice.*

## Lime dressing

juice of 3 limes

1 teaspoon honey

1 clove chopped garlic

1 chopped red chilli (optional)

1 teaspoon fish sauce

2 teaspoons soy sauce

Prepare the lime dressing by combining all the ingredients. Set aside. Preheat the oven to 220°C (450°F).

Remove the lobster heads and cut the tails in half lengthways. Place in a shallow baking tray along with the olive oil, wine and seasoning. Toss the lobsters in the liquid to ensure each one is well coated. Bake in the oven for 10–12 minutes until the meat is tender and the shells have turned bright red. Serve 2 lobster halves per person, accompanied with the bean shoots and watercress leaves on the side and drizzled with the lime dressing.

Serves 4

# Whole steamed river trout with wok-tossed bok choy and oyster mushrooms

4 whole fresh trout, cleaned

3 spring onions, sliced

2 cloves garlic, chopped

1 bunch parsley leaves

1 tablespoon lemongrass, chopped

1 lime, cut into wedges

sea salt and pepper to taste

2 cloves garlic, crushed

4 bok choy, washed and halved

250g (9oz) oyster mushrooms

½ cup (125ml/4fl oz) chicken stock

1 tablespoon oyster sauce

½ teaspoon sesame oil

fresh lime wedges, to garnish

Make three vertical slashes on each side of the trout. Combine the spring onions, garlic, parsley, lemongrass and lime wedges. Stuff the cavity of each trout with this mixture and place the fish on a steaming rack. Season well with sea salt and pepper, cover and steam each fish over a high heat for 15 minutes until cooked through.

Meanwhile, stir-fry the garlic, bok choy and oyster mushrooms in the chicken stock and oyster sauce until just heated through. Add a dash of sesame oil at the end and serve immediately alongside the fish. Garnish with fresh lime wedges.

Serves 4

# Poached white fish with lemon-scented garden herbs and ratatouille

4 x 185g (6½oz) white fish fillets
6 cups (1.5 litres/2½ pints) hot chicken stock
2 tablespoons chopped parsley
2 tablespoons chopped chives
1 teaspoon coriander, chopped
grated zest of 1 lemon
sea salt and freshly ground black pepper

### Ratatouille

1 cup (250ml/8fl oz) chicken stock or water
1 red onion, finely diced
2 cloves garlic, crushed
2 zucchini, finely diced
1 red capsicum, finely diced
1 yellow capsicum, finely diced
4 tomatoes, peeled, seeded and diced
sea salt and pepper to taste

First make the ratatouille. Sauté the onion and garlic with a little stock or water until soft. Add the zucchini, capsicums, tomatoes and the remaining stock and cook for a further 5–8 minutes. Season to taste and keep warm.

Place the fish fillets into a shallow pan and pour over the stock. Poach over a gentle heat for 5–7 minutes until cooked through. Combine the herbs, lemon zest, salt and pepper. Remove the fish from the stock and sprinkle with the herb mixture. Spoon some ratatouille onto each plate and top with a piece of fish. Serve immediately.

Serves 4

# Poached chicken breasts with cabbage, broccoli and cauliflower

4 skinless chicken breasts
½ savoy cabbage, cut into 4 wedges
¼ cauliflower, broken into florets
2 heads broccoli, cut into florets
250g (9oz) shiitake mushrooms, sliced
4 cups (1 litre/1½ pints) chicken stock
2 tablespoons low-salt soy sauce, to serve
chives, to garnish

Place the chicken and vegetables in a large pan and add the stock. Bring to the boil, cover and simmer gently for 10 minutes until the vegetables and chicken are tender. Ladle the vegetables and stock into serving bowls. Remove the chicken and slice. Place slices over the vegetables. Drizzle over a little soy sauce. Garnish with chives and serve immediately.

Serves 4

# Low-carbohydrate chilli beef burritos

¼ cup (60ml/2fl oz) low-salt soy sauce
¼ cup (60ml/2fl oz) mirin
2 cloves garlic, crushed
1 teaspoon ginger, finely chopped
1 teaspoon sesame oil
good grind of black pepper
500g (17½oz) fillet steak, thinly sliced
2 onions, sliced
1 red chilli, finely chopped
250g (9oz) mushrooms, sliced
1 red capsicum, sliced
2 spring onions, sliced
2 tablespoons coriander, chopped
iceberg lettuce leaves, to serve

Combine the soy sauce, mirin, garlic, ginger, sesame oil and black pepper. Add the steak, cover and marinate in the refrigerator for about 2 hours. Remove the meat from the marinade and sauté in a hot pan along with the onions, chilli, mushrooms and capsicum. Add a little of the leftover marinade, or a little water, as you cook. To finish, add the spring onions and coriander. To serve, spoon the beef filling into iceberg lettuce leaves and roll up. Serve immediately. (For variation, try substituting the beef with chicken, seafood or tempeh.)

Serves 4

# Smoked salmon with green sesame noodles

200g (6½oz) green tea noodles
2 tablespoons dried wakame seaweed, soaked in hot water for 3 minutes and drained
2 spring onions, sliced
2 tablespoons coriander, chopped
1 teaspoon olive oil
1 tablespoon soy sauce
100g (3½oz) smoked salmon
watercress leaves, to garnish
grated zest of 1 lemon, to garnish

Cook the noodles in plenty of boiling water until al dente. Drain well and add the seaweed, spring onions, coriander, olive oil and soy sauce. Toss and divide between serving plates. Arrange the smoked salmon over the top and garnish with the watercress leaves and lemon zest. (In this recipe, fresh or tinned salmon can be substituted for smoked.)

Serves 2

# Oysters with cucumber and lemon salad

1 cucumber, peeled and finely diced
juice and zest of 1 lemon
2 tablespoons finely chopped coriander
1 tablespoon low-salt soy sauce
1 teaspoon honey
4 dozen fresh opened oysters
lots of ice, to serve
freshly ground black pepper

Combine the cucumber, lemon juice and zest, coriander, soy sauce and honey. Arrange the oysters onto bowls of ice and place a little of the salad on top. Grind over some black pepper and serve immediately.

Serves 4

# Sardine fillets with lemon, black pepper and roasted sweet potatoes

2 large sweet potatoes, sliced
3 teaspoons olive oil
sea salt and black pepper
2 tablespoons balsamic vinegar, plus extra for serving
1 teaspoon fresh chopped rosemary
500g (17½oz) sardine fillets
juice of 2 lemons
2 tablespoons chopped parsley
rocket leaves, to garnish
lemon wedges, to serve

Preheat the oven to 200°C (400°F). Combine the sweet potatoes, 1 teaspoon olive oil, salt, pepper, balsamic vinegar and rosemary in a mixing bowl and toss well. Arrange on a baking tray and bake for about 35–40 minutes until the sweet potato is crisp and tender.

Meanwhile, 5 minutes before serving, heat the remaining olive oil in a non-stick, heavy-based pan. Season the sardine fillets and sauté in batches for 1 minute until cooked through.

Drizzle with lemon and sprinkle with parsley.

To serve, arrange the roast sweet potato on serving plates and pile on the sardine fillets.

Garnish with rocket leaves and lemon wedges. Drizzle with extra balsamic vinegar and serve.

Serves 4

# Fish cakes with cucumber salsa

250g (9oz) canned salmon, drained
2 cups (500g/17½oz) mashed potato
1 cup (155g/5½oz) sweet corn kernels, cooked
4 tablespoons chopped parsley
2 spring onions, sliced
2 cloves garlic, chopped
½ teaspoon lime zest
sea salt and ground black pepper, to taste
2 free range egg whites, beaten
2 cups (220g/8oz) fresh breadcrumbs

## Cucumber salsa

1 Lebanese cucumber, seeded and diced
2 tablespoons chopped coriander
juice of 1 lime
2 teaspoons fish sauce
pinch of sugar
1 red chilli, finely diced and seeded
ground black pepper, to taste

Combine all the salsa ingredients and set aside. Fold the salmon into the mashed potato along with the sweet corn kernels, parsley, spring onions, garlic, lime zest and seasoning. Form into 4 small cakes and refrigerate for 1 hour until firm. Dip each fish cake in the beaten egg whites and coat with breadcrumbs.

Heat a little olive oil in a pan and lightly fry until golden and cooked through. For thicker cakes, it is a good idea to finish them off for a few minutes in a hot oven to make sure they are well heated through. Serve with the cucumber salsa.

Serves 4

# Poached baby barramundi with stir-fried witlof and water chestnuts

2 x medium whole barramundi (or any white fish), cleaned and heads removed
2 cups (500ml/16fl oz) hot chicken stock
1 teaspoon peanut oil
3 witlof, washed and separated
1 green capsicum, sliced
125g (4½oz) water chestnuts, sliced
2 cloves garlic, crushed
1 tablespoon low-salt soy sauce

Gently poach the barramundi in the stock for 7–10 minutes until cooked through. Turn off the heat and allow to rest in the stock while preparing the remaining ingredients.

Heat the peanut oil in a non-stick pan and, when very hot, stir-fry the witlof with the capsicum and water chestnuts until the witlof is just wilted but still crisp. Add the garlic and soy sauce. Spoon onto serving plates and place the fish on the side. Serve immediately.

Serves 2

# Lean barbecued chicken burgers

500g (17½oz) lean chicken breast mince
2 spring onions, sliced
1 teaspoon sea salt and a good grind of black pepper
2 cloves garlic, crushed
1 teaspoon allspice
2 tablespoons chopped parsley
1 teaspoon olive oil
4 slices wholegrain bread, toasted
4 tablespoons barbecue sauce
1 Lebanese cucumber, thinly sliced lengthways using a vegetable peeler
2 ripe tomatoes, sliced
handful of green leaves
handful of bean shoots

Combine the mince, spring onions, salt, pepper, garlic, allspice and parsley. Form into 4 patties. Heat the olive oil in a non-stick pan and cook the patties over a medium heat for about 7–8 minutes until cooked through.

To serve, place half a piece of toast on each serving plate and top with barbecue sauce and cucumber ribbons. Add the chicken burgers and tomato. Top with the beanshoots and green leaves. Serve immediately. (For a low-carbohydrate meal, omit the toast and serve with extra salad.)

Serves 4

# Rice noodles tossed with crab, tomato and chilli

280g (10oz) freshly cooked soft rice noodles
280g (10oz) crab meat (about 3–4 whole crabs)
2 ripe tomatoes, diced
1 red chilli, chopped
juice of 2 limes
2 spring onions, sliced
2 cloves garlic, crushed
1 teaspoon sesame oil
1 teaspoon fish sauce
1 tablespoon low-salt soy sauce
freshly ground black pepper, to taste
lime wedges, to garnish

Place the noodles in a large serving bowl. Add the rest of the ingredients and mix well. Divide between two bowls and serve, garnished with lime wedges.

Serves 2

# Baked fish in banana leaf with fragrant yellow rice

1 onion, diced

2 cloves garlic, peeled

zest and juice of 2 limes

2 tablespoons chopped coriander

½ cup (125ml/4fl oz) reduced-fat coconut milk

sea salt and pepper, to taste

4 x 185g (6½oz) white fish fillets

4 large banana leaves or squares of aluminium foil

## Yellow rice

2 cups (370g/13oz) Jasmine rice

3 cups (750ml/24fl oz) water

pinch of salt

1 teaspoon turmeric

Preheat the oven to 200°C (400°F). Combine the onion, garlic, lime juice and zest, coriander and coconut milk in a food processor and process until blended. Taste for seasoning and adjust as necessary. Place the fish fillets in a dish and pour over the coconut marinade. Marinate in the refrigerator for about 30 minutes.

Blanch the banana leaves in boiling water for a few minutes to make them more pliable, then place a fish fillet on each leaf (or piece of aluminium foil) topped with some of the marinade. Wrap securely into parcels and tie with string. Place on a baking tray and cook in the oven for about 12–15 minutes until the fish is cooked through.

Meanwhile, heat the remaining marinade and prepare the yellow rice. Wash the rice in a sieve until the water runs clear, place in a saucepan and add the remaining ingredients. Cover and bring to the boil then turn the heat to low and allow the rice to simmer for 15–20 minutes until all the liquid has been absorbed and the rice is tender.

To serve, place the fish parcels on serving plates and remove the string. Accompany with yellow rice. Garnish with lime wedges and coriander leaves.

Serves 4

# Baked salmon steaks with udon noodles and coriander lime pesto

4 x 155g (5½oz) salmon steaks
315g (11oz) udon noodles
lime wedges, to serve

### Coriander lime pesto

1 bunch fresh coriander leaves
juice of 1 lime
2 cloves garlic, crushed
grind of black pepper and pinch of sea salt
6 tablespoons cold-pressed extra virgin olive oil
4–6 tablespoons chicken stock
2 tablespoons pine nuts, toasted

Preheat the oven to 200°C (400°F). First make the pesto by combining all the ingredients in a food processor and processing until smooth (add more olive oil if necessary). Set aside. Season the salmon steaks with a little salt and black pepper and place on a foil-lined baking tray. Bake in the oven for 10 minutes until cooked through.

Meanwhile, cook the noodles in plenty of boiling salted water until al dente then drain well. Mix the pesto through the noodles and divide between serving plates. Top with the salmon steaks and garnish with fresh lime wedges. Serve immediately.

Serves 4

# pure

fresh,
clean
flavours

# Ocean trout mille feuille with tomato and avocado salsa

4 sheets filo pastry
1 free range egg white
1 tablespoon sesame seeds
185g (6½oz) smoked ocean trout, thinly sliced
sea salt and pepper
lemon and lime wedges, to garnish

### Salsa

½ avocado, chopped
2 tomatoes, chopped
½ cucumber, peeled, seeded and diced
2 cloves garlic, crushed
2 spring onions, sliced
juice of 1 lime
pinch of sugar
sea salt and pepper to taste

Preheat the oven to 200°C (400°F). Divide each sheet of filo pastry in half and brush with egg white. Sprinkle with sesame seeds and gently scrunch up. Arrange on a baking tray and cook for 12–15 minutes until golden. Cool.

Make the salsa by combining all the ingredients, then set aside. To assemble, arrange a piece of filo on each serving plate. Top with a few slices of ocean trout and spoon over a little salsa. Finish with another layer of filo. Season to taste and garnish with lime and lemon wedges and serve immediately, accompanied with low-fat mayonnaise (see p. 158).

Serves 2

# Marinated tuna steaks with oven-roasted whole tomatoes and warm bean salad

½ cup (125ml/4fl oz) water
½ cup (125ml/4fl oz) salt-reduced soy sauce
¼ cup (60ml/2fl oz) mirin
juice of 1 lemon
4 x 185g (6½oz) tuna steaks
4 whole sun-ripened tomatoes, cored
1 teaspoon olive oil
sea salt and pepper, to taste
½ teaspoon ginger
2 cloves garlic, crushed
¼–½ cup (60ml/2fl oz–125ml/4fl oz) chicken stock
250g (9oz) green beans
220g (8oz) broad beans, peeled
2 spring onions, sliced
2 tablespoons chopped coriander
1 teaspoon olive oil

**MIRIN** *is a sweetened Japanese rice wine used only for cooking.*

Preheat the oven to 200°C (400°F). Combine the water, soy sauce, mirin and lemon juice. Add the tuna steaks and marinate in the fridge for about 15–30 minutes. Meanwhile, cut a small cross on top of the tomatoes and place on a baking tray. Drizzle with the olive oil and season with salt and pepper. Bake in the oven for about 15–20 minutes.

Sauté the ginger and garlic in a little of the chicken stock for a few seconds, then add the beans and cook with the remaining stock until just tender. Add the spring onions and coriander, and season with salt and pepper.

Heat a non-stick pan until hot, but not smoking. Add the olive oil and sear the tuna for 1–2 minutes on each side, adding some of the marinade to form a light sauce for the dish. The tuna should be nice and pink in the centre. To serve, divide the beans between serving plates and top each with a roasted tomato. Place the tuna to the side and drizzle with a little sauce.

Serves 4

# Roasted tomato and mushroom pizza

4 large portabello mushrooms, stems removed
sea salt and freshly ground pepper
1 teaspoon olive oil
1 large red onion, finely diced
2 cloves garlic, crushed
3 anchovies, finely chopped
1 red capsicum, finely diced
1 tablespoon chopped fresh basil
1 tablespoon chopped parsley
2 ripe roma tomatoes, quartered
4 bocconcini, sliced
rocket leaves, to garnish
balsamic vinegar, to serve

BOCCONCINI *are small balls of mozzarella cheese preserved in whey.*

Preheat the oven to 200°C (400°F). Peel the outer skin from the mushrooms and place on a baking tray.

Season with salt and pepper and set aside.

Heat the olive oil in a non-stick pan and sauté the onion and garlic until soft. Add the anchovies and

capsicum and cook for a few minutes until softened. Add the basil and parsley and season to taste.

Fill the mushroom cavities with the mixture.

Place two tomato quarters on each mushroom followed by the sliced bocconcini. Season well and

bake in the oven for 20–25 minutes until golden. Place on serving plates and garnish with rocket leaves.

Drizzle with a little balsamic vinegar and serve immediately.

Serves 4

# Teriyaki cod fillet with broad beans and verve dressing

220g (8oz) shelled broad beans
½ cup (125ml/4fl oz) chicken stock
4 x 185g (6½oz) cod fillets
4 tablespoons teriyaki or oyster sauce

### Verve dressing

4 tablespoons chopped coriander
2 tablespoons chopped chives
1 spring onion, sliced
1 clove garlic, crushed
2 tablespoons lime juice
1 tablespoon soy sauce
1 teaspoon honey
ground black pepper
1 teaspoon olive oil

First make the dressing by combining all the ingredients, then set aside. Cook the beans in the chicken stock until tender and the liquid has almost evaporated. Add the dressing, mix and set aside. Cook the cod fillets in a non-stick pan with a little stock or water until cooked through (about 5 minutes). Add the teriyaki sauce and turn the cod fillets to coat. Spoon the broad beans onto serving plates and top with the fish.

Serves 4

# Sesame-crusted roasted pork fillet with buckwheat soba noodles

500g (17½oz) trimmed pork loin

sea salt and ground black pepper

2 tablespoons sesame seeds

1 teaspoon olive oil

400g (14oz) buckwheat soba noodles

3 sheets nori seaweed, cut into thin strips with scissors

1 red capsicum, diced

1 red chilli, seeded and diced

4 tablespoons soy sauce

1 teaspoon sesame oil

snow pea sprouts, to garnish

---

Preheat the oven to 160°C (320°F). Season the pork loin with salt and pepper and coat with sesame seeds. Heat the olive oil in a pan and sear the pork until browned all over. Transfer to a roasting pan and roast in the oven for about 30 minutes until cooked. Allow to rest for about 8 minutes before serving.

Meanwhile, cook the noodles in plenty of boiling water. Add the nori strips then drain immediately. Transfer to a bowl and add the capsicum, chilli, soy sauce and sesame oil. Divide between serving bowls. Slice the pork loin and arrange on top. Garnish with snow pea sprouts.

Serves 4

# Mushroom linguini

300g (10½oz) linguini pasta

2 onions, finely diced

3 cloves garlic, crushed

750g (1lb 6½oz) assorted mushrooms, including button, shiitake, oyster and portabello

½ cup (125ml/4fl oz) vegetable or chicken stock

2 bunches chives, finely chopped

sea salt and pepper to taste

2 tablespoons freshly grated parmesan cheese

---

Cook the pasta in plenty of salted boiling water until al dente. Meanwhile, sauté the onion and garlic in a little stock until soft. Add the mushrooms and cook until soft and golden (about 5 minutes), adding a little stock as necessary. Add the chives and season with salt and pepper. Mix the mushrooms and hot pasta with the parmesan cheese. Serve immediately.

Serves 4

# Chilli squid salad

3 tubes cleaned squid, scored and cut into portions
1 red chilli, chopped
2 tablespoons fish sauce
4 tablespoons soy sauce
juice of 1 lime
1 teaspoon sesame oil
½ red capsicum, sliced
½ yellow capsicum, sliced
2 spring onions, sliced
2 witlof, washed and separated
lime wedges, to serve

Combine the squid with the chilli, fish sauce, soy sauce, lime juice and sesame oil. Marinate in the refrigerator for 30 minutes, then sauté in a hot non-stick pan for 1 minute until tender. Add the capsicums, spring onions and warm through. Serve over the witlof leaves.

Serves 2

# Mussels poached in Thai aromatics with rice noodle salad

1 teaspoon sesame oil
1 onion, finely diced
2 cloves garlic, chopped
1 teaspoon lemongrass, finely chopped
½ cup (125ml/4fl oz) chicken stock
500g (17½oz) fresh live mussels, scrubbed and beards removed
4 tablespoons chopped coriander
coriander leaves, to garnish
lemon or lime wedges, to garnish

### Rice noodle salad
juice of 2 limes
1 teaspoon honey
2 cloves garlic, crushed
½ red chilli, seeded and finely chopped
2 tablespoons low-salt soy sauce
2 teaspoons fish sauce
280g (10oz) cooked rice noodles, drained
250g (9oz) bean sprouts
handful of watercress leaves
2 spring onions, sliced

First make the rice noodle salad. Mix the lime juice with the honey, garlic and chilli. Add the soy sauce and fish sauce and set aside. Place the noodles, bean sprouts, watercress and spring onions in a bowl. Pour over the dressing and toss well. Divide between serving bowls and set aside while you prepare the mussels.

Heat the sesame oil in a pan and sauté the onion, garlic and lemongrass until golden. Add the chicken stock and bring to the boil. Add the mussels, then cover and simmer for 5 minutes until opened. Discard any mussels that remain closed. Mix through the coriander and spoon into 2 large serving bowls. Serve immediately with the rice noodle salad, garnished with fresh herbs and lemon or lime wedges.

Serves 2

# Silken tofu with greens and shiitake mushrooms in oyster sauce

1 teaspoon olive oil

2 cloves garlic, crushed

½ cup (125ml/4fl oz) vegetable or chicken stock

250g (9oz) shiitake mushrooms, sliced

2 bunches English spinach leaves, washed

2 witlof, separated into leaves

2 tablespoons oyster sauce

315g (11oz) silken tofu

snow pea sprouts, pickled ginger and

bean sprouts, to garnish

---

Heat a non-stick pan until hot. Add the olive oil and sauté the garlic with a little of the vegetable or chicken stock until soft. Add the mushrooms and cook for 1 minute. Add the spinach leaves and witlof and cook until just wilted, adding a little stock as necessary. Add the oyster sauce and toss to combine. Divide between serving plates.

Cut the tofu into 4 pieces and place over the greens. Garnish with the combined sprouts, ginger and bean sprouts.

Serves 4

# Poached seafood in lime and coconut dressing

400g (14oz) mixed fresh seafood (e.g. prawns, scallops, fish)

500ml (2 cups/16fl oz) chicken stock

1 spring onion, sliced

2 tablespoons chopped coriander

1 tablespoon finely chopped mint

juice of 2 limes

½ cup (125ml/4fl oz) low-fat coconut milk

1 tablespoon soy sauce

2 cloves garlic, crushed

1 red chilli, seeded and diced

¼ cup shredded lettuce

---

Poach the seafood in the stock until just cooked, about 1–2 minutes. Place in a bowl of iced water to cool. Meanwhile, combine the remaining ingredients (except the lettuce) in a bowl. Drain the seafood and add to the dressing. Toss to combine, then cover and marinate in the refrigerator for a minimum of 4 hours. To serve, place some lettuce at the base of each serving bowl and pile over the seafood. Serve immediately.

Serves 2

# Tonic soup

155g (5½oz) butterfly pasta (farfalle)
8 cups (2 litres/3½ pints) freshly made chicken
stock (see recipe, p. 156)
155g (5½oz) fresh garden peas
155g (5½oz) fresh broad beans, shelled
sea salt and pepper, to taste

Cook the pasta in plenty of salted boiling water until al dente. Drain and cool under cold running water. Bring the chicken stock to the boil in a saucepan. Add the peas and broad beans and cook for 2 minutes. Add the pasta and season with salt and pepper. Ladle into bowls and serve immediately.

Serves 4

# Chicken noodles

220g (8oz) glass noodles (bean thread noodles)
440g (15oz) poached chicken breast, finely chopped
3 cloves garlic, crushed
250g (9oz) shiitake mushrooms
1 red onion, finely diced
1 red capsicum, sliced
1 yellow capsicum, sliced
1 red chilli, seeded and finely diced
1 bunch coriander leaves, roughly chopped
3 tablespoons fish sauce
juice of 2 limes
4 tablespoons low-salt soy sauce
2 tablespoons chopped roasted cashew nuts (optional)

Soak the glass noodles in boiling water for

10 minutes. Drain, then rinse under cold running

water and drain again. In a large bowl, combine the

noodles with the rest of the ingredients. Toss well

and divide between 4 serving bowls.

Serves 4

# Wok-tossed prawns and vegetables

16 raw king prawns, shelled and deveined with tails intact

2 cloves garlic, crushed

½ teaspoon finely grated ginger

1 cup (250ml/8fl oz) chicken stock

8 asparagus spears, halved

4 bok choy, halved

250g (9oz) shiitake mushrooms, sliced

250g (9oz) oyster mushrooms

4 spring onions, sliced

2 tablespoons oyster sauce

1 tablespoon sweet soy sauce (*kecap manis*)

½ teaspoon sesame oil

Sauté the prawns, garlic and ginger in a hot wok with a little chicken stock for 1–2 minutes.

Add the asparagus, bok choy and mushrooms and sauté for a further minute, adding more

chicken stock if necessary. Then add the spring onions, oyster sauce, sweet soy sauce and

sesame oil. Cook for a further minute then spoon into serving bowls. Serve immediately.

**Serves 4**

# Inside-out sushi

2 cups (300g/10½oz) short grain white rice
3 cups (750ml/2¼ pints) water
2 tablespoons rice vinegar
2 teaspoons sugar
1 teaspoon sea salt
1 sheet nori seaweed
4 tablespoons toasted sesame seeds
½ avocado, cut into strips
1 cucumber, cut into long strips
1 red capsicum, sliced
low-salt soy sauce and wasabi paste, to serve

Wash the rice well, rubbing the grains against each other until the water runs clear, then drain. Place the rice and water in a saucepan and allow to stand for about 30 minutes. Place a lid on the saucepan, bring to the boil then simmer over a low heat for about 10 minutes. Do not remove the lid or stir the rice. Remove from the heat and allow the rice to stand for a further 10 minutes. Dissolve the sugar and salt in the vinegar.

In a non-metallic bowl, gently combine the rice with the vinegar mixture. Leave to cool to room temperature.

To assemble the sushi, place a sheet of nori on a work surface. Spread the cooked rice over the whole sheet, pressing it down firmly, and sprinkle with the sesame seeds. Carefully turn over the nori sheet, using both hands, so that the rice is face down. Arrange the strips of avocado, cucumber and capsicum in the middle of the nori sheet. Starting with the edge closest to you, roll up the nori sheet (so that the rice is on the outside of the roll) and wrap in plastic wrap. Carefully adjust the shape to form a neat cylinder. Remove the plastic wrap and cut into 6–8 portions. Serve with soy sauce and wasabi.

Serves 4

# Green tea noodles with garlic prawns

400g (13oz) green tea buckwheat noodles (*cha soba*, available from Japanese grocers)

2 tablespoons dried wakame

16 raw king prawns, peeled and deveined with tail intact

1 teaspoon sesame oil

3 cloves garlic, crushed

sea salt and pepper

juice of ½ lemon

2 tablespoons soy sauce

1 teaspoon olive oil

ground black pepper, to taste

Cook the noodles in plenty of boiling salted water until almost al dente, then add the wakame and boil for a further minute to reconstitute the dried seaweed.

Meanwhile, heat a large non-stick frying pan over a high heat and sauté the prawns in the sesame oil and garlic until the prawns have turned pink and are just cooked through. Season with salt and pepper and squeeze over the lemon juice.

Drain the noodles and wakame, place in a bowl and add the soy sauce and olive oil. Season well with ground black pepper and divide between four serving plates. Top each plate of noodles with four prawns and serve immediately.

Serves 4

# Lemongrass risotto with asparagus and pan-seared scallops

1 teaspoon olive oil
1 onion, finely chopped
1 stick lemongrass, finely chopped
1 cup (370g/13oz) arborio rice
4 cups (1 litre/1¾ pints) hot chicken stock
1 yellow capsicum, finely diced
½ cup (125ml/4fl oz) low-fat coconut milk
freshly ground sea salt and pepper to taste
12 scallops
16 asparagus spears

Sauté the onion and lemongrass in the olive oil until soft. Add the rice and stir through for 1 minute. Add half the stock and stir with a wooden spoon over a medium heat until the liquid is almost absorbed. Add the capsicum and the rest of the stock. Cook, stirring, over a medium heat until rice is cooked through and creamy, about 20–25 minutes. Just before serving, fold through the coconut milk then season well with salt and pepper. Sauté the scallops and asparagus in a little olive oil until just cooked and season well.

Divide the risotto between four serving bowls and top each bowl with the asparagus spears and scallops. Serve hot.

Serves 4

# Carrot and turmeric soup

2kg (4½lb) carrots, chopped
2 onions, chopped
8 cups (2 litres/3½ pints) vegetable or chicken stock
2 teaspoons fresh grated turmeric
5cm piece kombu seaweed (optional)
ground black pepper to taste

Place the carrots, onions, stock, turmeric and kombu in a large saucepan and bring to the boil. Cover loosely and simmer for 30 minutes until the carrots are soft. Remove from the heat. Remove the kombu, slice and set aside. Place batches of the mixture in a food processor or blender and blend until smooth. Adjust the consistency by adding more or less stock to the blender if necessary.

Return the blended soup to the saucepan and reheat. Season with black pepper and add the sliced kombu. Ladle into soup bowls and serve immediately.

Serves 6

# Green tea noodle sushi with cucumber, avocado and wasabi mayonnaise

400g (14oz) green tea soba noodles
½ teaspoon sesame oil
½ teaspoon grated ginger
6 sheets nori seaweed
1 avocado
1 Lebanese cucumber
6 shiitake mushrooms, thinly sliced

**Wasabi mayonnaise**
2 tablespoons soy mayonnaise
½ teaspoon wasabi paste

Cook the noodles in plenty of boiling salted water until al dente. Drain and rinse under cold water to cool. Drain again and toss with the sesame oil and ginger. Allow to rest at room temperature for 15 minutes.

Combine the mayonnaise ingredients and set aside. Peel the avocado, cut into quarters, then cut each quarter in half. Peel the cucumber, remove the seeds and cut into thin slices the same length as the nori sheets.

To assemble the sushi, place a sheet of nori on a bamboo mat and arrange some noodles on top, covering only half of the sheet. Spread 1 teaspoon mayonnaise over the noodles. Arrange slices of avocado, cucumber and mushroom on top of the noodles. Roll up the sushi firmly using the bamboo mat, then repeat with the remaining sushi sheets. Cut each nori roll into 6–8 portions and serve with soy sauce and picked ginger.

Serves 6

# Poached chicken and vegetables in broth

6 cups (1.5 litres/2½ pints) chicken stock
2 cloves garlic, crushed
500g (17½oz) chicken breast, sliced
1kg (2lb 2oz) mixed seasonal vegetables (e.g. Chinese cabbage, broccoli, celery, bok choy, spring onions, spinach, baby corn, shiitake mushrooms, wakame seaweed)
3 tablespoons soy sauce

Put the stock, garlic and sliced chicken breast in a pan and bring to the boil. Turn down the heat and simmer gently for 5 minutes until the chicken is cooked. Add the vegetables, cover and simmer for a further 8 minutes. Stir through the soy sauce and spoon into large serving bowls. Serve alone or with steamed jasmine rice.

Serves 4

# Lemon chicken with zucchini spaghettini

1 teaspoon olive oil
1 onion, sliced
3 cloves garlic, crushed
4 skinless chicken breasts
juice of 2 lemons
zest of 1 lemon
1 teaspoon honey
sea salt and pepper to taste

## Zucchini spaghettini

2 medium-sized green zucchini
2 medium-sized yellow zucchini
2 teaspoons olive oil
2 cloves garlic, chopped
4 tablespoons chopped parsley
sea salt and pepper to taste

Heat the olive oil in a frying pan and sauté the onion, garlic and chicken breasts on both sides until cooked and golden, adding a little water to keep the chicken tender. Once the water has evaporated, add the lemon juice, zest and honey. Keep warm.

Meanwhile, slice the zucchini using a mandolin to form 'spaghettini'. Blanch briefly in boiling water until tender (about 1 minute). Drain well. Heat the olive oil in a pan and sauté the garlic. Add the zucchini, toss through the parsley, and season. Divide between serving plates and top each serving with a chicken breast.

Serves 4

# Gazpacho with avocado lime salad

1.5 kg (3lbs 3oz) ripe tomatoes, peeled, seeded and chopped

2 cloves garlic, crushed

1 red chilli, chopped

½ red onion, chopped

1 red capsicum, diced

1 Lebanese cucumber, peeled, seeded and chopped

1 cup (250ml/8fl oz) tomato juice

3 tablespoons freshly chopped parsley

1 tablespoons freshly chopped coriander

sea salt and freshly ground black pepper

coriander leaves, to garnish

## Salad

1 avocado, chopped

½ Lebanese cucumber, peeled, seeded and finely chopped

juice of 2 limes

1 tablespoon chopped coriander

2 spring onions, sliced

Blend together the tomatoes, garlic, chilli, onion, capsicum, cucumber and tomato juice in a food processor until smooth. Fold through the fresh herbs and season well with salt and freshly ground black pepper. Refrigerate until cold.

To make the salad, simply combine all the ingredients in a bowl. To assemble the dish, place a round biscuit cutter in the centre of each serving bowl and fill with the salad. Pour the chilled gazpacho around the biscuit cutter, then remove the biscuit cutter. Garnish with coriander leaves and serve immediately.

Serves 6

# wholesome

hearty,
warming
food

# Pumpkin, spinach and lentil curry

2 onions, chopped

3 tablespoons red curry paste (see p. 157)

4 cups (1 litre/1½ pints) vegetable stock

½ cup (125ml/4fl oz) low-fat coconut milk

625g (1¼ lb) pumpkin, cut into chunks

2 carrots, grated

1 cup (200g/7oz) red lentils

2 bunches spinach leaves, washed

coriander, to garnish

---

In a large, deep pan, sauté the onion with

a little water until softened. Add the curry

paste and cook for a further minute.

Add the stock, coconut milk, pumpkin,

carrots and lentils. Cover and cook over a

gentle heat for 20–25 minutes until tender,

adding more stock if necessary. Add the

spinach and cook for a further 3 minutes.

Spoon into serving bowls, garnish with

coriander and serve immediately.

Serves 4

# Fettuccini with Mediterranean flavours

1kg (2lb 2oz) roma tomatoes, quartered
500g (17½oz) mushrooms
2 yellow capsicums, diced
sea salt and pepper
500g (17½oz) fettuccini pasta
4 tablespoons chopped parsley
2 cloves garlic, crushed
zest and juice of 1 lemon
1 tablespoon cold-pressed olive oil
ground black pepper, to taste
2 tablespoons freshly shaved parmesan cheese

Preheat the oven to 220°C (425°F). Combine the tomatoes, mushrooms, capsicum, salt and pepper and place on a baking tray. Roast in the oven for 20–25 minutes.

Meanwhile, cook the pasta in plenty of salted boiling water until al dente. Drain well and transfer to a large bowl. Add the roasted vegetables, parsley, garlic, lemon zest and juice, cold-pressed olive oil, black pepper and parmesan. Toss well and serve immediately.

Serves 4–6

# Roasted vegetables with couscous

1 red onion, peeled and cut into large dice

2 red capsicums, thickly sliced

2 yellow capsicums, thickly sliced

1 zucchini, halved and thickly sliced

1 teaspoon olive oil

2 cloves garlic, crushed

1 teaspoon sweet paprika

sea salt and black pepper to taste

1 onion, finely diced

1 cup (250ml/8fl oz) vegetable or chicken stock

220g (8oz) instant couscous

2 tablespoons chopped parsley

Preheat the oven to 200°C (400°F). Combine the red onion, capsicums, zucchini, olive oil, garlic, paprika, salt and pepper. Roast in the oven for about 30 minutes until tender and golden.

Meanwhile, prepare the couscous. Sauté the onion in a deep non-stick saucepan with a little water until soft. Add the stock and bring to the boil. Add the couscous, stir and remove from the heat. Cover with a tight-fitting lid and let stand for about 5 minutes until the stock is absorbed. Mix through the roasted vegetables and parsley. Divide between serving plates and serve immediately.

Serves 4

# Fish and scallops en papillote

2 x 155g (5½oz) white fish fillets

2 tablespoons chopped parsley

6 scallops

sea salt and pepper to taste

2 x thin slices lemongrass

splash of dry vermouth

Preheat the oven to 200°C (400°F). Place the fish onto 2 large pieces of baking paper or aluminium foil. Sprinkle with the chopped parsley, then arrange the scallops on top. Season well with salt and pepper, then place a slice of lemongrass on each piece of fish. Drizzle over a little vermouth, then fold the paper or foil over, ensuring the edges are well-sealed. Bake in the oven for about 10–15 minutes until cooked.

Place the parcels onto serving plates, and serve with a large green salad or steamed vegetables and soy sauce.

Serves 2

# Vegetable laksa

1 onion, diced

3–4 tablespoons laksa paste (see p. 157)

1 red capsicum, sliced

1 yellow capsicum, sliced

250g (9oz) mushrooms sliced

155g (5½oz) shiitake mushrooms, sliced

6 cups (1.5 litres/2½ pints) vegetable
or chicken stock

155g (5½oz) sugar snap peas

155g (5½oz) baby corn

500g (17½oz) fresh, thick rice noodles

300g (10½oz) firm tofu, cut into cubes

1 cup (250ml/8fl oz) low-fat coconut milk

---

Sauté the onion and laksa paste over a
medium heat until soft. Add the capsicums,
mushrooms and stock and cook for a further
5 minutes. Add the sugar snap peas, corn, rice
noodles, tofu and coconut milk. Bring to the
boil and heat through until the noodles are
soft. Ladle into deep serving bowls and
serve immediately.

Serves 4

# Smoked salmon filled with green papaya and crab salad

2 cloves garlic, crushed

2 small green chillies, seeded and diced

1 teaspoon lemongrass, finely chopped

¼ cup (60ml/2fl oz) freshly squeezed lime juice

2 tablespoons fish sauce

1 tablespoon palm sugar or light brown sugar

1 medium dark green papaya, peeled, seeded and grated

4 tablespoons chopped coriander

½ cup (60g/2oz) finely sliced snow pea sprouts

1 cup (250g/9oz) crab meat (about 4 medium crabs)

500g (17½oz) thinly sliced smoked salmon

### Dressing

1 tablespoon lime juice

1 teaspoon honey

sea salt and pepper to taste

watercress leaves, to garnish

---

Combine the garlic, chilli, lemongrass, lime juice, fish sauce and palm or
brown sugar. Mix well until the sugar is dissolved. Add the papaya,
coriander, snow pea sprouts and crab meat. Mix well. Line 4–6 small
moulds or ramekins with plastic wrap, then line with slices of smoked
salmon to cover the inside of the mould. Fill with crab salad and seal with
more salmon on top. Turn out onto serving plates and garnish with
watercress leaves. Drizzle with the combined lime juice, honey, salt and
pepper and serve.

Serves 4–6

# Silken tofu with avocado and lime

4 small lettuce leaf 'cups'

4 x 155g (5½oz) blocks silken tofu

½ avocado, cut into quarters

1 lime, cut into wedges

## Dressing (optional)

juice of 2 limes

1 teaspoon honey

2 cloves garlic, crushed

1 tablespoon fish sauce

Place the lettuce 'cups' onto serving plates and add a piece of tofu, avocado and a lime wedge. Combine the dressing ingredients and spoon over the tofu just before serving.

Serves 4

the anti-ageing cookbook

wholesome

# Pan-seared prawns in tandoori spices with cucumber sambal

2 cloves garlic, crushed

1 teaspoon finely chopped ginger

½ teaspoon ground cumin

½ teaspoon turmeric

1 teaspoon garam masala

1 teaspoon ground coriander

1 teaspoon chilli powder

1 tablespoon lemon juice

¾ cup (185ml/6fl oz) plain low-fat yoghurt

500g (17½oz) prawns, shelled and deveined with tails intact

## Cucumber sambal

1 cucumber, peeled, seeded and finely diced

sea salt to taste

½ cup (125ml/4fl oz) plain low-fat yoghurt

---

Combine all the ingredients except the prawns and mix well. Add the prawns and toss to coat. Leave to marinate in the refrigerator for about 30 minutes. Cook the prawns with a little olive oil in a heated non-stick frying pan for 5 minutes until the flesh has turned pink and is cooked through.

Meanwhile, combine the sambal ingredients and set aside. Serve the prawns with steamed basmati rice and cucumber sambal.

Serves 4

# Red wine, chicken and vegetable hot pot

500g (17½oz) skinless chicken breast pieces

60g (2oz) lean bacon, sliced

4 cloves garlic, crushed

1 onion, diced

3 cups (750ml/1¼ pints) chicken stock

1 tablespoon plain flour

1 cup (250ml/8fl oz) red wine

2 carrots, peeled and sliced

12 baby potatoes, peeled

300g (10½oz) mushrooms, sliced

1 teaspoon fresh thyme leaves

sea salt and pepper, to taste

---

Brown the chicken, bacon, garlic and onions in a little stock. Add the flour and stir to mix through. Pour in the red wine and remaining stock, followed by the carrots, potatoes, mushrooms and thyme. Cover and simmer gently for 30–40 minutes until the carrots and potatoes are tender. The sauce should be rich and thick.

Season with salt and pepper and spoon into serving bowls. Garnish with chopped parsley and serve. (For a low-carbohydrate meal omit the potatoes and substitute extra vegetables, e.g. zucchini.)

Serves 4

# Bigos

1 savoy cabbage, finely shredded

2 onions, finely diced

2 cloves garlic, chopped

500g (17½oz) skinless chicken breast, diced

1 cup (250ml/8fl oz) chicken stock

2 carrots, peeled and grated

1 x 440g (15½oz) can sauerkraut, well drained

2 bay leaves

sea salt and pepper, to taste

4 tablespoons chopped fresh parsley, to garnish

---

Preheat the oven to 180°C (350°F). Fill a large saucepan with water and bring to the boil. Add the cabbage and stir until wilted then drain well, squeezing out as much moisture as possible.

Sauté the onion and garlic in a non-stick frying pan with a little water or stock until soft and golden. Add the chicken and cook using a little stock until browned. Remove and transfer to a large casserole dish. Add the cabbage, carrot, sauerkraut and bay leaves and season well. Mix well until combined. Cover with foil and bake in the oven for 45 minutes to 1 hour. Serve hot, garnished with fresh herbs.

Serves 4–6

# Wok-seared broccolini with steamed yellow rice

2 cups (370g/13oz) jasmine rice

1 cup (250ml/8fl oz) water

1 cup (250ml/8fl oz) low-fat coconut milk

pinch of salt

pinch of sugar

1 pandan leaf (optional)

2 onions, sliced

3 cloves garlic, chopped

1 cup (250ml/8fl oz) vegetable stock

3 bunches broccolini, trimmed and washed

2 tablespoons low-salt soy sauce

---

Combine the rice, water, coconut milk, salt, sugar and pandan leaf in a pan and bring to the boil. Stir once only then cover. Turn down the heat and simmer gently for about 20 minutes until the rice grains are tender. Remove from the heat and leave for a further 5–10 minutes. Discard the pandan leaf.

Meanwhile, in a non-stick frying pan, sauté the onion and garlic in a little stock until golden. Add the broccolini and continue cooking for 3 minutes until tender, adding more stock as necessary. Add the soy sauce. To serve, spoon the rice into serving bowls and top with the broccolini. Serve immediately.

Serves 4

# Lime and soy marinated mackerel fillets with potato and watercress mash

4 x 185g (6½oz) pieces mackerel fillet

4 tablespoons low-salt soy sauce

juice of 2 limes

1 teaspoon sesame oil

¼ cup (60ml/2fl oz) water

5 large potatoes, peeled and chopped

1 teaspoon sea salt

½ cup (125 ml/4fl oz) light coconut milk

30g (1oz) watercress leaves, chopped

2 tablespoons chopped coriander

salt and ground black pepper, to taste

Combine the mackerel, soy sauce, lime juice and sesame oil and water in a bowl and marinate

in the refrigerator for 1 hour.

Place the potatoes in a saucepan and cover with cold water. Add the sea salt and bring to the boil.

Cook for 30 minutes until tender. Drain well. Shake the saucepan with the potatoes over a low heat for

1 minute to allow any excess water to evaporate, then mash the potato with the coconut milk until it

has a good, smooth consistency. Add the watercress and coriander leaves and season to taste.

Cook the mackerel in a heated non-stick frying pan with a little olive oil until cooked through. To serve,

dollop mash onto serving plates and top with mackerel. Serve immediately.

Serves 4

# Brown rice, soy bean and mushroom risotto

1 onion, finely diced

2 cloves garlic, chopped

2 cups (370g/13oz) short grain brown organic rice

6 cups (1.5 litres/2½ pints) hot vegetable
or chicken stock

1 tablespoon dried wakame

90g (3oz) oyster mushrooms, sliced

250g (9oz) button mushrooms, sliced

155g (5½oz) shiitake mushrooms, sliced

90g (3oz) black fungus, chopped

125g (4½oz) canned additive-free soy beans

4 tablespoons chopped coriander

2 tablespoons low-salt soy sauce

2 spring onions, sliced

ground black pepper, to taste

**BLACK FUNGUS** *is available from good greengrocers and Asian supermarkets.*

Sauté the onion and garlic in a little water until golden. Add the rice and cook, stirring, for 1 minute.

Add the stock and wakame and stir frequently with a wooden spoon over a low heat until the rice

is tender (about 30–40 minutes). Add more stock or water if necessary.

Meanwhile, in a separate pan, sauté the mushrooms and fungus in a little stock until soft.

Mix in the rice, miso, soy beans, coriander, soy sauce, spring onions and black pepper.

Divide between serving bowls and serve immediately.

Serves 6

# Wok-tossed green tea noodles with mushrooms and poached oysters

1 onion, finely diced

2 cloves garlic, chopped

155g (5½oz) oyster mushrooms

155g (5½oz) shiitake mushrooms, sliced

185g (6½oz) green tea noodles, cooked and drained

2 tablespoons wakame seaweed, soaked in hot water, drained and chopped

1 teaspoon sesame oil

1 tablespoon soy sauce

1 cup (250ml/8fl oz) water

½ cup (125ml/4fl oz) low-salt soy sauce

¼ cup (60ml/2fl oz) mirin

1 dozen oysters, shelled

Sauté the onion and garlic with a little water until soft. Add the mushrooms and cook until soft and golden, adding a little water if necessary. Add the noodles, wakame, sesame oil and soy sauce and heat through.

Meanwhile, heat the water, soy sauce and mirin in a small pan. Add the oysters and gently poach until warmed through, about 30 seconds.

To serve, divide the noodles between serving plates and top with the oysters. Drizzle over a little poaching liquid. Serve immediately.

Serves 2

# Butterfly pasta tossed with greens and ricotta

400g (14oz) butterfly pasta (farfalle)

220g (8oz) shelled green peas

220g (8oz) shelled broad beans

250g (9oz) smooth low-fat ricotta

2 tablespoons white wine

2 tablespoons grated parmesan cheese

2 cloves garlic, crushed

1 tablespoon shredded basil leaves

freshly ground black pepper

2 tablespoons chopped walnuts

Cook the pasta in plenty of boiling salted water until almost al dente.

Add the peas and broad beans and cook for a further 2 minutes.

Meanwhile, mix the ricotta with ¼ cup of the pasta water, and add the

wine, parmesan and garlic. Drain the pasta, peas and beans and place

on a serving dish. Add the ricotta mixture, basil, black pepper and walnuts

and mix until combined. Serve immediately.

Serves 4

# Chunky minestrone

1 onion, diced
2 cloves garlic, chopped
1 cup (125g/4½oz) sliced mushrooms
2 zucchini, diced
2 large carrots, diced
1 stick celery, diced
½ cup (100g/3½oz) red lentils
2 cups (500ml/16fl oz) chicken stock
1 x 440g (15½oz) can crushed tomatoes
1 cup (150g/5oz) peas
1 cup (150g/5oz) sweet corn kernels
sea salt and pepper, to taste
4 tablespoons freshly chopped herbs (e.g. parsley, basil)

---

Sauté the onion, garlic and mushrooms in a little water or stock until soft. Add the zucchini, carrot, celery, lentils, stock and tomatoes. Bring to the boil then simmer for 30 minutes. Add the peas and corn and simmer for a further 5 minutes. Season to taste and add the freshly chopped herbs just before serving.

Serves 4

# Red and yellow capsicum soup

6 red capsicums, halved and core removed
6 yellow capsicums, halved and core removed
1 onion, diced
6 cups (1.5 litres/2½ pints) chicken or vegetable stock
sea salt and freshly ground black pepper
crusty sourdough bread and avocado, to serve

---

Preheat the oven to 200°C (400°F). Place the capsicum halves skin side up on a foil-lined baking tray. Roast in the oven for 15–20 minutes until the capsicums have collapsed and the skin has wrinkled. Remove from the oven and allow to cool, then remove the skin.

Sauté the onion in a little water until softened. Blend the red capsicums in a food processor with half the stock and half the sautéed onion until smooth. Season well and set aside. Repeat with the yellow capsicums and the remaining stock and onion. To serve, reheat both soups separately and, using two ladles, pour both soups into a bowl at the same time (so that the bowl contains red soup on one side and yellow on the other). Serve immediately with crusty sourdough bread spread with avocado.

Serves 4

# Buckwheat noodles with shiitake mushrooms and poached ocean trout

6 cups (1.5 litres/2½ pints) chicken stock

1 stalk lemongrass, roughly chopped

1 teaspoon sliced ginger

4 x 185g (6½oz) ocean trout fillets

400g (14oz) buckwheat noodles

250g (9oz) shiitake mushrooms, sliced

3 spring onions, sliced

1 teaspoon sesame oil

2 tablespoons soy sauce

2 tablespoons chopped coriander

2 tablespoons wakame seaweed, soaked in hot water for 5 minutes and drained

snow pea sprouts and bean shoots, to garnish

---

Heat the stock, lemongrass and ginger, then simmer for 5 minutes to allow the flavours to infuse.

Add the ocean trout fillets and poach for 5 minutes until cooked through.

Meanwhile, cook the noodles in plenty of salted boiling water until al dente. Sauté the shiitake

mushrooms in a little chicken stock until softened. Drain the noodles and toss through the

mushrooms, spring onions, sesame oil, soy sauce, coriander and wakame. Divide the noodles

between four serving plates and top each with a poached ocean trout fillet. Serve immediately,

garnished with the combined snow pea sprouts and bean shoots.

Serves 4

# Seafood and chicken paella

4 single chicken breasts, cut into chunks
2 onions, diced
2 red chillies, chopped
4 cloves garlic, chopped
4 tomatoes, peeled and chopped
2 cups (370g/13oz) arborio rice
5 cups (1¼ litres/2 pints) hot chicken stock
2 teaspoons paprika
½ teaspoon saffron
250g (9oz) shelled green peas
250g (9oz) sweet corn kernels
1 red capsicum, diced
1 yellow capsicum, diced
500g (17½oz) raw prawns, deveined with tails intact
1kg (2¼ lbs) mussels, cleaned and bearded
splash of white wine (optional)
sea salt and pepper to taste
4 tablespoons freshly chopped parsley

Heat a large heavy-based saucepan for 2 minutes then brown the chicken in a little spring water until golden. Add the onion, chilli and garlic and cook for a further minute, then add the tomatoes and rice. Cook for a further 2–3 minutes, then add the stock, paprika and saffron. Cover and cook over a low heat until rice is almost tender.

Add the peas, corn, capsicums and seafood and mix through gently. Cover and continue cooking without stirring until the seafood is cooked and the rice is tender. Add more stock or a little white wine if necessary.

Just before serving, mix through the parsley and season to taste with salt and pepper.

Serves 8

# Lean zucchini lasagne

2 onions, diced

3 cloves garlic, chopped

2kg (4½lb) zucchini, grated

4 spring onions, sliced

2 tablespoons freshly chopped chives

2 tablespoons freshly chopped parsley

sea salt and pepper, to taste

1 packet fresh lasagne sheets or rice noodle sheets

250g (9oz) low-fat cheese, grated

## Bechamel sauce

1 onion, diced

1 leek, diced

1kg (2lb) low-fat cottage cheese

1–1½ cups (250ml/8fl oz–375ml/12fl oz) vegetable stock

sea salt and pepper, to taste

large crisp salad, to serve

Preheat the oven to 180°C (350°F). To prepare the sauce, sauté the onion and leek in a little water until soft. Spoon into a food processor or blender and add the cottage cheese and vegetable stock. Blend until smooth. Season with salt and pepper to taste.

To prepare the filling, sauté the onions and garlic in a little water until soft, then mix through the grated zucchini. Add the spring onions and herbs and season with salt and pepper to taste.

To assemble the lasagne, smooth a little of the bechamel sauce over the base of a baking dish, then cover with sheets of lasagne or rice noodles. Spread over half the zucchini mixture and sprinkle with a third of the grated cheese. Add another layer of lasagne or rice noodle sheets and spoon over the remaining zucchini mixture. Sprinkle with another third of the grated cheese and add another layer of lasagne or rice noodle sheets. Top with the remaining bechamel sauce, followed by the last of the grated cheese. Bake in the oven for about 45 minutes until golden (cover with foil if overbrowning).

Serve hot with a large crisp salad.

Serves 6–8

# Steamed dumplings filled with chicken, sweet corn and spinach

280g (10oz) lean chicken breast mince
1 cup (155g/5½oz) cooked sweet corn kernels
1 bunch spinach leaves, washed, blanched and chopped
2 spring onions, sliced
1 teaspoon sesame oil
2 tablespoons soy sauce, plus extra for serving
1 teaspoon fish sauce
1 packet gow gee wrappers
finely diced capsicum, to garnish

**GOW GEE WRAPPERS** *are flat, circular pieces of dough, similar to pasta. They are available fresh or frozen.*

Place the chicken mince in a bowl and add the sweet corn kernels, spinach, spring onion, sesame oil, soy and fish sauces. Mix well to combine. Place about 1 teaspoon of the mixture into the centre of each gow gee wrapper, then fold each wrapper in half to form semi-circles. Seal the edges by pinching together firmly. Place in a steamer basket and steam for about 7 minutes until cooked through. Garnish with the capsicum and serve with extra soy sauce.

Serves 4

# Veggie burgers with chunky veggie chips and tzatziki

180g (6oz) red lentils

2 cups (500ml/16fl oz) spring water

sea salt and pepper to taste

1 raw zucchini, grated

1 raw carrot, grated

2 spring onions, sliced

2 cloves garlic, chopped

1 stick celery, finely diced

2 tablespoons chopped walnuts

2 tablespoons chopped parsley

2 free range egg whites

2 tablespoons wheat germ

## Veggie chips

2 sweet potatoes, washed and cut into wedges

2 carrots, peeled and cut into lengths

2 parsnips, peeled and cut into lengths

2 medium potatoes, washed and cut into wedges

1 tablepsoon olive oil

sea salt and pepper

1 teaspoon sweet paprika

2 cups tzatziki (see p. 158), to serve

crisp salad leaves, to serve

Preheat the oven to 200°C (400°F). Make the veggie chips by combining all the ingredients, then spread out on a large baking tray. Bake in the oven for 40 minutes or until golden.

Meanwhile, place the lentils and water in a saucepan and bring to the boil. Reduce the heat, cover and simmer for 30 minutes until the water has been absorbed and lentils are cooked. Allow to cool, then combine with the remaining burger ingredients. Shape into 10 patties then sauté in a non-stick frying pan with a little olive oil until golden brown.

Serve with crisp salad leaves, accompanied with vegetable chips and tzatziki.

Makes 10 burgers

# fresh

uplifting
fruit
desserts

# Summer puddings with melon salad

12–14 slices of bread, crusts removed
500g (17½oz) strawberries, quartered
1 punnet (250g/9oz) blueberries
1 punnet (250g/9oz) raspberries
1 cup (250ml/8fl oz) red wine
1 cup (250g/9oz) raw sugar
zest and juice of 1 lemon
zest and juice of 1 orange
2 teaspoons gelatine

## Melon salad
1 honeydew melon, peeled and sliced
¼ cup (60ml/2fl oz) Midori liqueur

Line 8 individual dariole moulds or small cups with plastic wrap, making sure some hangs over the edge. Next, line the moulds with the bread, making sure there are no gaps.

Place the fruit in a saucepan along with the red wine, sugar, and the citrus zest and juices. Stir over a gentle heat for 3 minutes until the juices have been released from the berries. Add the gelatine and stir until dissolved. Fill the moulds with the berry mixture, then cover the top with a circle of bread, ensuring it fits evenly. Pour the remaining juices over the puddings, then cover with the excess plastic wrap. Place the puddings on a tray and weigh down with a heavy plate. Chill for 4 hours or overnight.

Release the puddings from their moulds, removing the plastic wrap, and cut in half.

Arrange on top of the sliced melon and drizzle with Midori. Serve immediately.

Serves 8

fresh

# Lime and green tea tiramisù

500g (17½oz) low-fat quark (or cream cheese)
155g (5½oz) caster sugar
½ cup (125ml/4fl oz) lime juice
zest of 2 limes
1½ packets lime jelly crystals
1 teaspoon green tea powder
100ml (3fl oz) hot water
6 free range egg whites, beaten to soft peaks
1 packet sponge finger biscuits
1 cup (250ml/8fl oz) Midori liqueur
2 mangoes, sliced, to garnish

In a blender, process the cheese, sugar, lime juice and zest until smooth.

Dissolve the jelly crystals and green tea powder in the hot water, then add

to the cheese mixture and blend well. Pour the cheese mixture over the

beaten egg whites and gently fold through until combined. Line a long loaf tin

with 2 sheets of plastic wrap.

Dip the sponge fingers briefly into the Midori and arrange over the base of the

tin. Pour over just enough of the cheese mixture to cover the biscuits. Arrange

another layer of biscuits (dipped in the Midori) on top, followed by the cheese

mixture, and continue in this manner, finishing with a layer of biscuits. This will

make it easier for cutting and serving. Leave to set in the refrigerator overnight.

Garnish with mango slices and serve chilled with green tea wafers.

Serves 10

# Green tea wafers

85g (3oz) plain flour
½ teaspoon green tea powder
1 teaspoon grated lime zest
50g (2oz) icing sugar
30ml (1fl oz) macadamia nut or
grapeseed oil
1 free range egg white
1 tablespoon shaved coconut

Preheat the oven to 180°C (350°F).

Mix the flour, green tea powder, lime

zest, icing sugar, macadamia oil and

egg white until smooth. Spread thinly

onto a sheet of greaseproof paper

using a metal spatula. Sprinkle with

the shaved coconut then bake in the

oven for 8–10 minutes until golden.

Cool completely, then break into

pieces for a rustic effect.

# Pear, apricot and passionfruit crumble

4 pears, peeled, cored and sliced
3 tablespoons water
2 tablespoons raw sugar
1 teaspoon vanilla essence
pulp of 3 passionfruit
6 apricots, halved
90g (3oz) rolled oats
4 tablespoons maple syrup
1 tablespoon macadamia nut or grapeseed oil
1 tablespoon walnut halves
low-fat vanilla yoghurt, to serve

Preheat the oven to 180°C (350°F). Place the sliced pears, water, sugar and vanilla in a saucepan and cook for 5–8 minutes until the pears have softened. Remove from the heat and combine with the passionfruit and apricot halves. Divide between 4 individual heat-proof dishes and set aside.

Combine the oats, maple syrup, macadamia nut oil and walnut halves, then sprinkle over the pears. Bake in the oven for 20–30 minutes until golden. Serve warm with low-fat vanilla yoghurt.

Serves 4

# Lime, green tea and lemon sorbet

500g (17½oz) caster sugar
2 cups (500 ml/16fl oz) spring water
1 teaspoon green tea powder
¾ cup (190 ml/6fl oz) lemon juice
½ cup (125ml/4fl oz) lime juice
grated zest of 2 limes

Combine the sugar and water in a pot and bring to the boil. Stir until the sugar has dissolved and remove from the heat. Mix a little of the hot sugar syrup into the green tea powder to dissolve and add to the rest of the sugar syrup. Whisk in the lemon and lime juice, followed by the lime zest. Pour into an ice-cream maker and churn according to instructions or, alternatively, pour the mixture into a metal cake tin and freeze for 2½–3 hours, until just starting to firm up. Remove from the freezer and beat with an electric beater until smooth. Return to the freezer until the mixture is firm.

Serves 4

## Variations

### Mixed berry

Make the sugar syrup as for the lime and green tea sorbet.

In a blender, process 500g (17½oz) strawberries, 250g (9oz) blueberries and 250g (9oz) raspberries. Add half the sugar syrup and blend again until smooth, then add the mixture to the remaining sugar syrup. Add ¼ cup (60ml/2fl oz) lemon juice and mix well. Complete as for the lime and green tea sorbet.

### Mango and passionfruit

Make the sugar syrup as for the lime and green tea sorbet.

In a blender, process 750g (1½ lb) chopped mango with half the sugar syrup. Blend until smooth then add to the rest of the sugar syrup. Add ½ cup (125ml/4fl oz) lime juice and mix well. Complete as for the lime and green tea sorbet.

### Pink grapefruit and guava

Make the sugar syrup as for the lime and green tea sorbet, using only half the quantities. Whisk in 2 cups (500ml/16fl oz) pink grapefruit juice, followed by 2 cups (500ml/16fl oz) guava juice. Complete as for the lime and green tea sorbet.

# Strawberry romanoff

2 punnets (500g/17½oz) strawberries, washed, hulled and quartered
3 tablespoons orange liqueur (Cointreau or Grand Marnier)
2 tablespoons caster sugar
juice of 1 orange
220g (8oz) sugar
½ cup (125ml/4fl oz) spring water
3 free range egg whites
500g (17½oz) low-fat quark (or cream cheese)
2 teaspoons vanilla extract
juice and zest of 2 lemons
frosted rose petals, to garnish (optional)

Combine the strawberries, orange liqueur, caster sugar and orange juice in a bowl and leave to macerate for 30 minutes. Combine the sugar and water in a saucepan and bring to the boil. Attach a sugar thermometer. Without stirring, boil the sugar syrup until the temperature reaches 120°C (240°F). If you don't have a sugar thermometer, you can test the syrup by putting a few drops into a cup of cold water. The drops should feel soft but firm.

Meanwhile, beat the egg whites until soft peaks form, then slowly drizzle in the hot sugar syrup as you beat, until well combined. Continue beating on high speed for 6–8 minutes until cool. In another bowl, beat the quark, vanilla, lemon juice and zest until smooth. Fold through the egg whites. Make frosted rose petals by brushing the petals of 1 washed and dried rose with a little beaten egg white. Dip into caster sugar and place onto a plate to dry.

Divide the macerated strawberries between 8 serving glasses and spoon over the egg white topping. Garnish with rose petals just before serving.

Serves 8

# Warm baked stone fruits in red wine

4 peaches, halved
4 plums, halved
4 apricots, halved
1½ cups (375ml/12fl oz) red wine
3 tablespoons fructose
½ teaspoon ground cinnamon

Preheat the oven to 180°C (350°F). Place the fruits in individual ovenproof dishes. Pour over the red wine and scatter with fructose and cinnamon. Bake for 15–20 minutes until the fruits are soft and golden. Serve warm.

Serves 4

# Rhapsody in blue

4 cups (1 litre/1½ pints) spring water
1½ cups (375ml/12fl oz) blue Curaçao liqueur
½ cup (125ml/4fl oz) lemon juice
1 cup (200g/7oz) fructose
8 firm pears, peeled

Combine the water, Curaçao, lemon juice

and fructose in a saucepan and bring to the

boil. Add the pears, cover with a layer of

greaseproof paper and simmer over a gentle

heat for 30–40 minutes or until the pears are

tender (test with a skewer). Allow to cool in

the syrup then refrigerate until chilled.

Serves 8

# Nashi pears poached in chamomile with papaya salad

2 cups (500ml/16fl oz) spring water
¼ cup (60ml/2fl oz) pure honey
4 chamomile tea bags
4 nashi pears, peeled and quartered
250g (9oz) fresh papaya, diced
juice of 2 limes
1 teaspoon fructose

Place the water, honey and tea bags in a pan and bring to the boil. Remove from the heat and allow the tea to steep for 10 minutes. Remove the tea bags and return the pan to the heat. Add the nashi pears, cover loosely and simmer over a gentle heat for 10 minutes until tender. Remove from the heat and allow to cool, then chill in the refrigerator.

Meanwhile, combine the papaya, lime juice and fructose. To serve, spoon the nashi pears into serving bowls with some of the poaching liquid and spoon the papaya over the top.

Serves 4

# Fresh fruits in chardonnay syrup

1 bottle chardonnay
juice of 1 lemon
1¼ cups (250g/9oz) fructose
1 vanilla bean, halved lengthways
1 ripe pineapple, diced
1 ripe papaya, diced
2 mangoes, diced
4 kiwi fruit, sliced
2 punnets (500g/17½oz) strawberries, washed and hulled

Combine the chardonnay with the lemon juice, fructose and vanilla bean then bring to the boil. Simmer until the sugar has dissolved then remove from the heat. Place the chopped fruit in a serving bowl and pour over the warm syrup. Allow to cool then place in the refrigerator. Serve chilled.

Serves 10

# Chilled pineapple and papaya with coconut zabaglione

1½ cups (345g/12oz) pineapple chunks
1½ cups (345g/12oz) papaya chunks
1 free range egg
1 free range egg white
1 tablespoon fructose
1 teaspoon vanilla extract
pulp of 2 passionfruit
¼ cup (60ml/2fl oz) coconut liqueur
¼ cup (60ml/2fl oz) reduced-fat coconut milk

Combine the pineapple and papaya then divide between 4 serving glasses. Combine the remaining ingredients in a stainless steel bowl and place the bowl over a pan of simmering water. Whisk until the mixture starts to look thick and creamy. Remove from the heat and ladle over the fruit.

Serve immediately.

Serves 4

# Poached peaches with ginseng, green tea and lime

6 ripe peaches
4 cups (1 litre/1½ pints) spring water
1½ cups (375ml/12fl oz) pure honey
2 tablespoons Japanese green tea, or 3 tea bags
2 tablespoons ginseng tea, or 3 tea bags
juice of 4 limes

Plunge the peaches in boiling water for 30 seconds, remove the skin and refresh in a bowl of iced water. Combine the spring water, honey and teas in a pan and bring to the boil. Remove from the heat and infuse the tea for 8–10 minutes, then strain into a clean pan. Bring to the boil, then add the lime juice and skinned peaches. Reduce the heat and simmer for 5 minutes. Remove from the heat and allow to cool in the poaching syrup, then chill in the refrigerator.

To serve, place the peaches in martini glasses and spoon over the chilled syrup.

Serves 6

# Berry and red wine trifle

1 bottle red wine (e.g. merlot)
½ cup (100g/3½oz) fructose
grated zest of 1 orange
grated zest of 1 lemon
2 sticks cinnamon
500g (17½oz) strawberries, washed and hulled
1 punnet 250g (9oz) raspberries
2 punnets 500g (17½oz) blueberries
2 cups (500ml/16fl oz) thick low-fat vanilla yoghurt

Place the red wine, fructose, orange and lemon zest and cinnamon in a saucepan and bring to the boil. Reduce the heat and simmer for 15–20 minutes until the wine is reduced by half. Remove from the heat. Place the berries in a heatproof bowl and pour over the hot syrup. Allow to cool at room temperature then refrigerate until chilled. Assemble in martini glasses, alternating layers of the berry compote and the yoghurt, finishing off with the berry compote.

Serves 8

# Red and white poached pears

## Red pears

1 litre (1½ pints) unsweetened dark grape juice

zest of 1 orange

6 firm pears, peeled

## White pears

1 litre (1½ pints) unsweetened apple juice

zest of 2 lemons

6 firm pears, peeled

Prepare the red and white pears simultaneously, in two separate saucepans. Add the grape juice and orange zest to one saucepan, and the apple juice and lemon zest to the other. Bring both to the boil, then turn down the heat to a low simmer. Add 6 pears to each pan. Cover each pan loosely with a circle of greaseproof paper and simmer gently for 40 minutes, or until a skewer is easily inserted into the pears. Remove the pears from the hot liquid and set aside. Simmer the remaining liquid in each saucepan until reduced by half to form a rich sauce. Remove from the heat and return the pears to the two saucepans. Refrigerate until chilled.

To assemble, slice each pear thickly horizontally and arrange on plates, alternating the red and white layers. Spoon over a little of each sauce and serve immediately.

For variation, replace the dark grape juice with 1 bottle red wine and 1½ cups (375g/13oz) caster sugar, and the apple juice with 1 bottle white wine and 1½ cups (375g/13oz) caster sugar.

Serves 6

# comfort

soothing
sweet
food

# Rhubarb crumble

4 stems rhubarb, chopped, leaves discarded

2 apples, peeled and chopped

grated zest and juice of 1 orange

½ cup (125g/4½oz) raw sugar

2 tablespoons desiccated coconut

2 tablespoons chopped macadamia nuts

6 tablespoons rolled oats

pinch of cinnamon

2–3 tablespoons pure maple syrup

2 teaspoons macadamia nut or grapeseed oil

low-fat vanilla yoghurt, to serve

---

Preheat the oven to 180°C (350°F). Place the rhubarb, apples, orange juice, zest and sugar in a saucepan and simmer over a low heat for 10–15 minutes until tender. Cool and divide between 4 individual heatproof dishes. Combine the remaining ingredients and sprinkle over the rhubarb. Bake in the oven for 25–30 minutes until golden. Serve warm with low-fat vanilla yoghurt.

Serves 4

# Chunky apple strudel

6 Granny Smith apples, peeled and diced

3 tablespoons raw sugar

2 tablespoons pure honey

pinch of cinnamon

pinch of ground cloves

zest and juice of 1 lemon

90g (3oz) fresh breadcrumbs

2 tablespoons ground almonds

6 sheets filo pastry

2 tablespoons macadamia nut or grapeseed oil

low-fat yoghurt, to serve

---

Preheat the oven to 180°C (350°F). Combine the apples, sugar, honey, spices, lemon zest and juice, breadcrumbs and ground almonds. Mix well. Place 2 sheets of filo on a non-stick baking tray and brush lightly with a little macadamia oil. Repeat this procedure with the other 4 sheets of filo. Spoon the apple mixture onto the centre of the pastry to form a log shape. Roll up, tucking the ends underneath. Brush with a little more oil and bake in the oven for 25 minutes until the pastry is crisp and golden. Serve warm with low-fat yoghurt.

Serves 6

# Sticky rice pudding with mango

1 cup (185g/6½oz) short-grain rice

2 cups (500ml/16fl oz) water

pinch of salt

1 pandan leaf (optional)

2–3 tablespoons fructose

¾ cup (180ml/6fl oz) lite coconut milk

2 teaspoons vanilla extract

1 mango, peeled and cut into quarters

Combine the rice, water, salt and pandan leaf in a pan.

Cover and bring to the boil. Turn down the heat and

simmer gently for 15–20 minutes until tender. Remove

from the heat and fold through the fructose, coconut

milk and vanilla. Leave to rest for 10–15 minutes.

Serve either warm or chilled with mango.

Serves 4

# Carrot cake with lemon cheesecake frosting

3 carrots, finely grated
2 free range eggs
4 free range egg whites
1 teaspoon salt
2 teaspoons vanilla extract
½ cup (125ml/4fl oz) macadamia nut or grapeseed oil
1 cup (250ml/8fl oz) apple sauce
1½ cups (375g/13oz) raw sugar
1 cup unsweetened crushed pineapple
1½ cups (375g/13oz) wholemeal organic flour
1½ cups (375g/13oz) unbleached organic plain flour
2 teaspoons baking powder
¾ cup (90g/3oz) walnuts
2 tablespoons rolled oats

### Frosting

500g (17½oz) low-fat quark (or cream cheese)
4–5 tablespoons fructose
zest of 1 lemon
2 tablespoons lemon juice
glacé ginger pieces, to decorate (optional)

Preheat the oven to 180°C (350°F). In a large bowl, combine the carrots, eggs, salt, vanilla, oil, apple sauce, sugar and pineapple. Fold in the flours, baking powder and walnuts and mix well. Spoon into a baking tray oiled with macadamia nut oil and coated with the rolled oats. Bake in the oven for 40–50 minutes until cooked through. Cool in the tin for 20 minutes before turning out onto a wire rack.

Meanwhile, make the frosting by beating all the ingredients together until smooth. Spread the cake with the frosting or serve on the side.

Makes 1 cake

# Chocolate beetroot cake with raspberry sauce

6 large egg whites
1¾ cups (270g/9½oz) dark brown sugar
pinch of sea salt
2 teaspoons vanilla extract
2 cups (500ml/16fl oz) red wine, reduced over a
low heat to ½ cup (125ml/4fl oz)
½ cup (125ml/4fl oz) macadamia nut or
grapeseed oil
2 cups (400g/14oz) finely grated beetroot
2 cups (250g/9oz) organic plain flour
2 teaspoons baking powder
½ cup (45g/1½oz) good quality cocoa powder
½ cup (60g/2oz) finely chopped brazil nuts
icing sugar, to dust

## Raspberry sauce

500g (17½oz) raspberries
juice of 2 oranges
1 tablespoon fructose

Preheat the oven to 170°C (340°F). Beat the egg whites until soft peaks form. Add the sugar a little

at a time, beating well after each addition. Add the salt and vanilla and continue beating until the

egg whites are light, smooth and fluffy. Fold in the reduced red wine, oil, beetroot, flour, baking

powder, cocoa powder and brazil nuts and mix until well combined. Pour into a baking tin oiled

with a little macadamia nut oil and dusted with cocoa powder. Bake for about 30–40 minutes. (To

test if the cake is cooked, insert a skewer into the cake. If it comes out clean, the cake is cooked.)

Cool in the tin for 15 minutes, then turn out onto a baking tray and leave to cool completely.

Meanwhile, make the sauce by blending the raspberries with the orange juice and fructose.

Strain. Dust the cake with icing sugar and serve with raspberry sauce.

Serves 12

comfort

# Banana and passionfruit crème brûlée with mango salad

1 large banana, mashed

juice of ½ lime

1 x 170g (6oz) can passionfruit in syrup

250g (9oz) silken tofu

1 tablespoon coconut milk powder

1 tablespoon honey (optional)

½ mango, peeled and chopped

2 tablespoons caster sugar

---

In a food processor, blend the banana, lime juice,

passionfruit, tofu, coconut milk powder and honey

until smooth. Divide the mango between

2 heatproof dishes. Top with the banana and

passionfruit mixture and cover with plastic wrap.

Chill for at least 1 hour. To serve, sprinkle the top of

each brûlée with the sugar and grill under a high

heat for 1 minute (or use a kitchen blowtorch) until

the sugar has caramelised. Serve immediately.

Serves 2–4

# Sliced bananas with honey nut crumble

1 ripe banana, peeled

juice of 1 lime

1 teaspoon honey

2 teaspoons toasted desiccated coconut

1 tablespoon chopped cashew nuts

1 tablespoon chopped brazil nuts

---

Coat the banana with lime juice and brush with

honey. Combine the coconut and nuts and roll the

banana in this mixture. Slice into 4 thick pieces

and serve alone or with low-fat yoghurt.

Serves 1

# Upside-down lemon and blueberry syrup puddings

155g (5½oz) organic plain flour
1 teaspoon baking powder
pinch of salt
100g (3½oz) raw sugar
zest and juice of 1 lemon
2 tablespoons macadamia nut or grapeseed oil
¼ cup (60ml/2fl oz) low-fat coconut milk
1½ cups (375ml/12fl oz) pure maple syrup
500g (17½oz) blueberries

Preheat the oven to 180°C (350°F). In a bowl, combine the flour, baking powder, salt, sugar, lemon zest and juice, oil and coconut milk. Mix lightly and set aside. Lightly oil 6 soufflé dishes. Pour some maple syrup into each dish, then divide the blueberries between the dishes. Spoon in the lemon mixture and bake in the oven for 25 minutes until golden. Cool for 5–10 minutes before turning out to serve.

Serves 6

# Lime and coconut pie with pistachio nut crust

6 cups (180g/6oz) cornflakes

¼ cup (60ml/2fl oz) desiccated coconut

2 tablespoons pistachio nuts

2 tablespoons cashew nut paste

2–3 tablespoons honey

1 x 440g (15½oz) can low-fat sweetened condensed milk

4 free range eggs

⅔ cup (160 ml/5fl oz) lime juice

zest of 3 limes

4 free range egg whites

5 tablespoons fructose

Preheat the oven to 165°C (330°F). Combine the cornflakes, desiccated coconut, pistachio nuts, cashew nut paste and honey in a food processor. Blend until the mixture sticks together when squeezed.

Line 10 muffins tins with greaseproof paper and divide a little of the cornflake mixture between each one. Press down to form a base and bring a little up the sides. Wet your hands with water if the mixture gets too sticky.

To make the filling, beat the condensed milk and eggs until combined. Add the lime juice and zest, then pour into the muffin tins. Bake in the oven for 20–30 minutes until set.

Beat the egg whites until soft peaks form, then gradually add the fructose as you continue beating until the mixture is smooth and glossy and the fructose has dissolved into the whites. Spoon on top of the pies and bake for a further 10 minutes until golden. Refrigerate before serving.

Serves 10

# Pumpkin pecan pie

6 cups (180g/6oz) cornflakes
½ cup (45g/1½oz) desiccated coconut
2 tablespoons pecan nuts, finely chopped
2 tablespoons cashew nut paste
2–3 tablespoons honey
750g (1½ lbs) pumpkin chunks, roasted and cooled
5 tablespoons pure maple syrup
juice and zest of 1 orange
2 teaspoons vanilla extract
½ teaspoon ground cinnamon
½ teaspoon ground nutmeg
3 free range egg whites
100g (3½oz) fresh dates, sliced
pecan nuts, to garnish

Preheat the oven to 165°C (330°F). Combine the cornflakes, coconut, pecan nuts, cashew paste and honey in a food processor. Blend until the mixture sticks together when squeezed.

Line 10 muffin tins with greaseproof paper and divide the cornflake mixture between the muffin tins. Press down to form a base and bring a little way up the sides. Wet your hands if the mixture gets too sticky.

Put the pumpkin, maple syrup, orange zest and juice, vanilla, spices and egg whites in a food processor. Process until well combined. Sprinkle the dates over the base of the pie shells and spoon over the pumpkin mixture. Top with the pecan nuts and bake in the oven for 20–30 minutes. Cool. Serve chilled or at room temperature.

Makes 10 individual pies

# Peach soufflé with berry compote

155g (5½oz) dried peaches
1 cup (250ml/8fl oz) water
3 tablespoons raw sugar
1 teaspoon vanilla extract
3 free range egg whites, beaten to soft peaks

**Berry compote**
1 punnet (250g/9oz) raspberries
juice of 2 oranges
1 tablespoon fructose
1 punnet (250g/9oz) strawberries, washed and quartered

Preheat the oven to 180°C (350°F). Combine the peaches, water, sugar and vanilla in a saucepan and simmer for 20 minutes, until most of the liquid has been absorbed and the peaches are moist and plump. Purée until the mixture is smooth. Cool. Fold in the beaten egg whites and spoon into 1 large or 6 small oiled and sugared soufflé dishes or cups. Place in a baking dish, then pour in cold water to reach halfway up the sides of the soufflé dishes. Bake in the oven for 15–20 minutes until puffed and golden.

Meanwhile, make the berry compote by blending the raspberries with the orange juice and fructose. Fold through the strawberries and set aside. Serve the peach soufflé accompanied with berry compote.

Serves 6

# Chewy no-bake fruit and nut cookies

2 cups (380g/13oz) mixed dried fruit (e.g. apricots, pears, peaches)
½ cup (60g/2oz) chopped walnuts
½ cup (60g/2oz) chopped brazil nuts
2 tablespoons pumpkin seeds
2 tablespoons sunflower seeds
juice and zest of 1 orange
1 cup (90g/3oz) desiccated coconut

Combine all the ingredients except the coconut in a food processor and process until combined. Form into small cookie-shaped balls with your hands or use a small ice-cream scoop. Roll half of the ball in desiccated coconut. Store, covered, in the refrigerator for up to 1 week.

Makes 30 cookies

comfort

# aqua

## hydrating, healing juices

# Purify
# and cleanse

All the fruits, vegetables and herbs used
in these drinks have cleansing properties
to flush out toxins from the body.

## Soothing lemongrass tea

1 whole lemongrass stem, chopped
4 cups (2 litres/1½ pints) boiling spring water

Put the lemongrass in a coffee plunger or
heatproof jug. Pour over the boiling water
and let stand for at least 15 minutes before
drinking. Serve warm, at room temperature
or chilled.

Serves 2

## Hydrating green juice

1 cup (250ml/8fl oz) freshly squeezed apple juice
¼ cup (60ml/2fl oz) freshly squeezed spinach juice
¼ cup (60ml/2fl oz) freshly squeezed watercress juice
30ml (1fl oz) freshly squeezed wheat grass juice

Combine all the freshly
squeezed juices and
drink immediately.

Serves 1

## Purifying punch

1 cup (250ml/8fl oz) carrot juice
½ cup (125ml/4fl oz) pear juice
¼ cup (60ml/2fl oz) beetroot juice
1 tablespoon turmeric juice

Combine all the ingredients
and drink immediately.

Serves 1

# Harmonising detox tonic

1 cup (250ml/8fl oz) chilled cucumber juice
½ cup (125ml/4fl oz) pear juice
juice of 1 lemon
¼ cup (60ml/2fl oz) green dandelion leaf juice
1 teaspoon mint juice
1 teaspoon parsley juice

Combine all the ingredients in a tall, chilled glass and drink immediately.

Serves 1

# Clarifying ruby cooler

½ cup (125ml/8fl oz) beetroot juice
½ cup (125ml/8fl oz) cranberry juice
¼ cup (60ml/2fl oz) cherry juice
¼ cup (60ml/2fl oz) raspberry juice
¼ cup (60ml/2fl oz) aloe vera juice

Combine all the ingredients in a tall, chilled glass and drink immediately.

Serves 1

# Revitalising thirst quencher

1 cup (250ml/8fl oz) red grape juice
½ cup (125ml/4fl oz) apple juice
juice of 1 lemon

Combine the freshly squeezed juices and drink immediately.

Serves 1

# Replenishing wheat grass shooter

¼ cup (60ml/2fl oz) wheatgrass juice

Juice the fresh green grass and drink immediately. (You can order fresh wheat grass trays from your local health food store, or you can grow your own. One large tray should last about a week.)

Wheat grass is the young sprouts of grains of wheat. It has high concentrations of chlorophyll, active enzymes, vitamins and minerals.

As well as being one of the richest natural sources of vitamin A, wheat grass also contains complex B group vitamins, vitamin C, vitamin E, calcium, potassium, iron, magnesium, phosphorus, sodium, sulphur, zinc and amino acids.

Wheat grass is a powerful cleansing agent as the chlorophyll brings toxins into the bloodstream that have been stored in the cells of fatty tissue. They are then released through the elimination processes in the body. The juice is best drunk on an empty stomach and can sometimes cause a little nausea. It is absorbed into the system in approximately 20 minutes, which makes it a great energiser. Because it is so nutritionally dense, it can curb the appetite, and has also been known to reduce the effects of body odour and bad breath.

the anti-ageing cookbook

151

aqua

# Energy and vitality

These drinks are packed with energy and goodness for hard-core movers and shakers.

## Uplifting watermelon and strawberry cooler

2 cups (440g/15½oz) chopped watermelon

½ punnet (125g/4½oz) strawberries, washed and hulled

½ cup (125ml/4fl oz) freshly squeezed apple juice

1 cup crushed ice

---

Combine all the ingredients in a blender and process until combined. Serve immediately.

Serves 1

## Nourishing papaya passionfruit drink

1 cup (220g/6½oz) chopped, peeled papaya

1 cup (250ml/8fl oz) freshly squeezed orange juice

pulp of 2 passionfruit

½ cup crushed ice

---

Combine all the ingredients in a blender and process until smooth. Serve immediately.

Serves 1

# Rejuvenating power blaster

1 cup (250ml/8fl oz) guava juice
1 ripe banana
250g (9oz) strawberries, washed and hulled
½ cup crushed ice

Combine all the ingredients in a blender and process until smooth. Serve immediately.

Serves 1

# The bionic mango energiser

1 cup (250ml/8fl oz) low-fat yoghurt with active cultures
1 mango, peeled and chopped
½ cup crushed ice

Combine all the ingredients in a blender and process until smooth. Drink immediately.

Serves 1

# Enriching peach banana rumba

1 banana, peeled and chopped
1 cup (250ml/8fl oz) peach juice
½ mango, chopped
juice of 1 lime
½ cup crushed ice

Combine all the ingredients in a blender and process until smooth. Serve immediately.

Serves 1

# Revitalising 'Brazilian' banana blender

1 cup (250ml/8fl oz) organic low-fat soy milk
1 ripe banana
1 tablespoon wheat germ
1 teaspoon ground brazil nuts
1 teaspoon honey
½ cup crushed ice

Combine all the ingredients in a blender and process until smooth. Drink immediately.

Serves 1

# Reviving iced ginseng tea

1 tablespoon loose leaf ginseng tea, or 3 tea bags
2 cups (500ml/16fl oz) hot filtered water
2 teaspoons honey
2 limes, cut into wedges
1 cup crushed ice, to serve

Place the tea in a coffee plunger and fill with hot filtered water. Allow to infuse for 10–15 minutes before straining into a heatproof jug. Stir in the honey, then cool and chill in the refrigerator. To serve, fill glasses with lightly squeezed lime wedges and ice then pour over the tea.

Serves 2

# Immunity and wellbeing

These drinks contain high sources of antioxidants, which help repair cell damage in the body, fighting illness and slowing the ageing process.

## Clarifying iced green tea with lime

1 tablespoon green tea leaves

2 tablespoons chopped mint leaves

juice and zest of 1 lime

2 teaspoons pure honey

2 cups (500ml/16fl oz) filtered boiling water

---

Put the tea, mint, lime zest and honey in a coffee plunger and pour over the boiling water. Steep for 10 minutes then strain into a heatproof jug. Chill in the refrigerator for 2 hours. Add the lime juice and serve poured over ice.

Serves 2

## Empowering red berry sangria

2 cups (500ml/16fl oz) good quality red wine (e.g. merlot)

2 cups (500ml/16fl oz) fresh apple juice

1 cup (250ml/8fl oz) sparkling mineral water

2 punnets (250g/9oz) mixed berries (e.g. strawberries, blueberries, raspberries)

ice, to serve

---

Mix the wine, apple juice and mineral water in a jug. Add the berries and ice and serve immediately.

Serves 2

# Replenishing beauty tonic

3 oranges

2 guava fruit

1 punnet (250g/9oz) strawberries, washed and hulled

1 cup chopped papaya

½ cup crushed ice

Juice the oranges and guavas then combine in a blender with the strawberries, papaya and ice. Blend until smooth and serve immediately.

Serves 1

# Fortifying hot chilli tomato drink

4 ripe red tomatoes

1 red capsicum

¼ red chilli, seeded

1 clove garlic

lemon wedge, to serve

sea salt, to serve (optional)

ice, to serve

celery, to garnish (optional)

Juice the tomatoes, capsicum, chilli and garlic in a juice extractor. Rub the edge of a serving glass with lemon and coat with a little sea salt. Add ice to the glass and pour over the juice. Serve immediately, garnished with a slice of lemon and small stick of celery.

Serves 1

# Restoring pink grapefruit and guava 'martini'

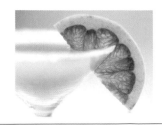

2 pink grapefruit

1 cup ice

½ cup (125ml/4fl oz) guava juice

1 small garlic clove, peeled

slice of grapefruit, to garnish

Squeeze the grapefruit and pour the juice into a cocktail shaker filled with ice. Pour over the guava juice. Stir for 1 minute then strain into a sugar-crusted martini glass. Skewer the garlic with a toothpick and add to the martini glass. Garnish with a slice of grapefruit and serve immediately. Take a few sips of the juice, eat the garlic clove then finish the juice.

Serves 1

# Multivitamin antioxidant booster

2 carrots, washed

½ head broccoli

1 red capsicum

1 pear

¼ cup (60ml/2fl oz) wheat grass juice

½ teaspoon ginger

Place all the ingredients in a juicer then serve immediately.

Serves 1–2

# Essential basic recipes

## Chicken stock

1kg (2lbs) chicken bones
3 litres (5 pints) cold water
1 onion, roughly chopped
1 carrot, roughly chopped
1 stick celery, roughly chopped
1 x 10cm piece kombu seaweed
3 sprigs parsley
1 sprig thyme
½ teaspoon whole black peppercorns
1 teaspoon sea salt
**Makes 2 litres (3 pints)**

Combine the chicken bones and water in a large saucepan. (For a brown stock, roast the chicken bones until very brown before adding to the stock pot.) Simmer slowly for 2 hours. Add the rest of the ingredients and simmer for 1 hour. Strain through a fine sieve and refrigerate. (Reduce the stock after straining to strengthen the flavour, if desired.) Before using, remove any fat that has solidified on the surface. Store in the refrigerator for up to 1 week, or freeze until needed.

### Variation

Use veal bones instead of chicken bones, but simmer for 6–7 hours, adding more water if necessary.

## Vegetable stock

2 litres (3¼ pints) water
2 onions, chopped
1 carrot, chopped
1 stick celery, chopped
2 cups (250g/9oz) mushrooms
1 x 10cm piece kombu seaweed
dash of white wine
½ teaspoon black peppercorns
1 teaspoon salt
**Makes 2 litres (3 pints)**

Combine all the ingredients in a large saucepan and simmer for 1 hour. Strain and cool. (Reduce the stock after straining to increase flavour, if desired.) Store in the refrigerator for up to 1 week, or freeze until needed.

## Basic tomato sauce

2 onions, finely chopped
2 cloves garlic, crushed
1kg (2lb) ripe tomatoes, peeled and chopped, or 2 x 440g (15½oz) cans crushed tomato
2 tablespoons tomato paste
1 teaspoon raw sugar
sea salt and black pepper, to taste
2 cups (500ml/16fl oz) chicken or vegetable stock
4 tablespoons freshly chopped parsley
**Makes 1 litre (1½ pints)**

Sauté the onions and garlic in a little water until golden. Add the tomatoes, tomato paste, sugar, seasoning and stock. Cover and simmer gently for 35–45 minutes until rich and thick. Add the parsley just before serving.

essential

# Green curry paste

1 teaspoon coriander seed
20 small green chillies
1 stem lemongrass, chopped
zest of 2 limes
5 cloves garlic, crushed
2 spring onions, sliced
1 teaspoon fresh ginger
1 teaspoon ground black pepper
Makes ½ cup (125ml/4fl oz)

Heat the coriander seeds in a non-stick pan for 1 minute to release the flavour. Place in a food processor or mortar with the remaining ingredients, and process or pound with a pestle until smooth. Add a little lime juice or water if the mixture is too dry. Store in an airtight container in the refrigerator for up to a month.

# Red curry paste

1 teaspoon coriander seeds
10 red chillies
1 stem lemongrass, chopped
1 tablespoon freshly chopped ginger
5 cloves garlic, crushed
zest of 2 limes
4 spring onions, sliced
2 teaspoons ground black pepper
Makes ½ cup (125ml/4fl oz)

Dry roast the coriander seeds in a non-stick pan for 1 minute to release the flavour. Place in a food processor or mortar with the remaining ingredients, and process or pound with a pestle until smooth. Store in an airtight container in the refrigerator for up to 1 month.

# Laksa paste

1 onion, chopped
1 tablespoon ginger, diced
4 cloves garlic, diced
2 stalks lemongrass, chopped
4 red chillies, seeded and chopped
1 tablespoon shrimp paste (optional)
2 teaspoons fresh chopped turmeric
1 teaspoon ground coriander
1 teaspoon ground cumin
Makes ¼ cup (60ml/4fl oz)

Blend all the ingredients in a food processor and store, covered, in the refrigerator for up to 5 days, or in the freezer for up to 6 months.

# Thai-style vinaigrette

½ cup (125ml/4fl oz) lime juice
1 tablespoon honey
1 clove garlic, crushed
1 tablespoon fish sauce
1 red chilli, chopped
1 tablespoon chopped coriander
Makes ½ cup (125ml/4fl oz)

Combine all the ingredients in a bowl and use over salads and vegetables.

## Tzatziki

2 cups (500ml/16fl oz) Greek style yoghurt
1 Lebanese cucumber, peeled, seeded and finely diced
1 tablespoon lemon juice
1 whole bulb garlic, roasted until soft
sea salt and pepper to taste
4 tablespoons chives, chopped
4 tablespoons coriander, chopped
Makes 2 cups (500ml/16fl oz)

Combine all the ingredients and refrigerate until needed for up to 3 days.

## Low-fat mayonnaise

1 cup (250ml/8fl oz) low-fat natural yoghurt
2 tablespoons smooth low-fat ricotta
3 tablespoons white wine vinegar
1 teaspoon Dijon mustard
sea salt and pepper, to taste
Makes 1½ cups (375ml/12fl oz)

Combine all the ingredients in a food processor and process until smooth. Refrigerate until needed for up to 3 days. To vary the flavour, add any of the following: freshly chopped herbs, capers, sliced spring onion, crushed garlic, Tabasco sauce, Worcestershire sauce, anchovies, wasabi.

## Wheat-free and gluten-free pastry

6 cups (185g/6½oz) gluten-free rice flakes or corn flakes
½ cup (45g/1½oz) desiccated coconut
1 tablespoon sunflower seeds
1 tablespoon pumpkin seeds
2 tablespoons cashew nut paste
2 tablespoons honey
1 free range egg white

Combine all the ingredients in a food processor and process until combined. The mixture should stick together when pressed. Use as required. For a savoury crust, omit the honey and add an additional 1 or 2 egg whites.

## Shortcrust pastry

220g (8oz) flour
pinch of sea salt
1 teaspoon baking powder
45g (1½oz) butter
125g (4oz) low-fat quark (or cream cheese)
1 free range egg white
2 tablespoons water
¼ cup (60g/2oz) icing sugar (optional, for a sweet pastry)

Combine all the ingredients in a food processor and process until the mixture forms a ball. Wrap in plastic wrap and allow to rest in the refrigerator for an hour before using.

# index